Also available from BBC Worldwide:

The Nation's Favourite Poems
ISBN: 0 563 38782 3
ISBN: 0 563 38487 5 (hardback gift edition)

The Nation's Favourite Love Poems
ISBN: 0 563 38378 X
ISBN: 0 563 38432 8 (hardback gift edition)

The Nation's Favourite Comic Poems
ISBN: 0 563 38451 4

The Nation's Favourite Twentieth Century Poems
ISBN: 0 563 55143 7

The Nation's Favourite Shakespeare
ISBN: 0 563 55142 9

The Nation's Favourite Poems of Childhood
ISBN: 0 563 55184 4

The Nation's Favourite Children's Poems
ISBN: 0 563 53774 4

The Nation's Favourite Poems of Animals
ISBN: 0 563 53780 9

The Nation's Favourite Poems of Journeys
ISBN: 0 563 53715 9

Audio cassettes available from BBC Radio Collection

The Nation's Favourite Poems
ISBN: 0 563 38987 7

The Nation's Favourite Love Poems
ISBN: 0 563 38279 1

The Nation's Favourite Comic Poems
ISBN: 0 563 55850 4

The Nation's Favourite Shakespeare
ISBN: 0 563 55331 6

The Nation's Favourite Lakeland Poems
ISBN: 0 563 55293 X

The Nation's Favourite Poems of Childhood
ISBN: 0 563 47727 X

The above titles are also available on CD

THE NATION'S FAVOURITE POEMS OF CELEBRATION

— ◇ —

FOREWORD BY

ROGER McGOUGH

Published by
BBC Worldwide Limited,
Woodlands,
80 Wood Lane,
London
W12 0TT

First published 2002
Edited and compiled by Alex Warwick,
Emma Shackleton and Sarah Lavelle
Compilation © BBC Worldwide 2002
Poems © individual copyright holders

ISBN: 0 563 48824 7

Set in Stempel Garamond by Keystroke,
Jacaranda Lodge, Wolverhampton.
Printed and bound in Great Britain by Martins the Printers Ltd,
Berwick-upon-Tweed.
Cover printed by Belmont Press, Northampton.

THE POETRY SOCIETY

The Poetry Society has been promoting poets and poetry in Britain since 1909.
A membership organisation open to all, it publishes Britain's leading poetry
magazine, *Poetry Review*, runs the National Poetry Competition, has a
lively education programme and offers advice and information on reading and
writing poetry. For further information telephone 020 7420 9880 or email
info@poetrysoc.com
www.poetrysoc.com

CONTENTS

— ◇ —

– Contents –

*'Now that I am fifty-six
Come and celebrate with me —'*

'Because I love'

– Contents –

'Such love I cannot analyse;
It does not rest in lips or eyes'

– Contents –

'Nice warm socks,
Nice warm socks—
We should celebrate them.'

'My heart leaps up when I behold
A rainbow in the sky'

– Contents –

FOREWORD BY ROGER McGOUGH

— ◇ —

Let us celebrate the pleasure of reading poetry.

Let us celebrate the act of writing it.

Let us celebrate the people who inspired the poems:
The lovers, the mothers, the mistresses and daughters.

Let us celebrate the seven buxom women abreast,
     staggering and sliding on the icy road
Let us celebrate the loudness of their laughter.

Let us celebrate the glory of the garden
The wild rose-briar where the bee sucks,
Apple-blossom and the nations of birds lifting together.

Let us celebrate landscape, for I like that stuff
The secret ministry of frost, full-moon & rainbows
Let us celebrate the heart that leaps up.

Let us celebrate walking in beauty like the night,
dappled things and the marriage of true minds.
Let us celebrate delicious babies, balloons and
the liquefaction of Julia's clothes.

Let us celebrate the Joy of Socks.
Love in the back of vans. Sing the body
reclining and the lolling breast.
And while we are at it, let us celebrate
the wet wooden squeegee handle poking out
of the bucket behind the red gas pump.

Let us celebrate this wondrous life we lead
Pass the tambourine, and let us bash out praises.

Let us celebrate the way we were and the way we live now.
Let us celebrate the way we will be
It's a joy to behold, getting old & wearing purple.

Let us celebrate the benediction of poetry
The writing, reading, singing and dancing of it.

Let us count the ways to celebrate.
Let us celebrate.

Roger McGough
July 2002

'It makes me laugh. In fact, it makes me sing.'

from 'Londoner'

WILLIAM SHAKESPEARE 1564–1616

WHERE THE BEE SUCKS,
THERE SUCK I

Where the bee sucks, there suck I:
In a cowslip's bell I lie;
There I couch when owls do cry.
On the bat's back I do fly
After summer merrily.
Merrily, merrily shall I live now
Under the blossom that hangs on the bough.

GRACE NICHOLS 1950–

THE BODY RECLINING
(With a thought for Walt)

I sing the body reclining
I sing the throwing back of self
I sing the cushioned head
The fallen arm
The lolling breast
I sing the body reclining
As an indolent continent

I sing the body reclining
I sing the easy breathing ribs
I sing the horizontal neck
I sing the slow-moving blood
Sluggish as a river
In its lower course

I sing the weighing thighs
The idle toes
The liming knees
I sing the body reclining
As a wayward tree

I sing the restful nerve

Those who scrub and scrub
incessantly
corrupt the body

Those who dust and dust
incessantly
also corrupt the body

And are caught in the asylum
Of their own making
Therefore I sing the body reclining

WALLACE STEVENS 1879–1955

THE HOUSE WAS QUIET AND THE WORLD WAS CALM

The house was quiet and the world was calm.
The reader became the book; and summer night

Was like the conscious being of the book.
The house was quiet and the world was calm.

The words were spoken as if there was no book,
Except that the reader leaned above the page,

Wanted to lean, wanted much most to be
The scholar to whom his book is true, to whom

The summer night is like a perfection of thought.
The house was quiet because it had to be.

The quiet was part of the meaning, part of the mind:
The access of perfection to the page.

And the world was calm. The truth in a calm world,
In which there is no other meaning, itself

Is calm, itself is summer and night, itself
Is the reader leaning late and reading there.

JAMES BERRY 1924–

BENEDICTION

Thanks to the ear
that someone may hear

Thanks to seeing
that someone may see

Thanks to feeling
that someone may feel

Thanks to touch
that one may be touched

Thanks to flowering of white moon
and spreading shawl of black night
holding villages and cities together

IRVING FELDMAN 1928–

YOU KNOW WHAT I'M SAYING?

'I favor your enterprise,' the soup ladle says.
'And I regard you and your project with joy.'

At Grand Forks where the road divides twice over,
the wet wooden squeegee handle poking out
of the bucket beside the red gas pump tells you,
'*Whichever* way – hey, for you they're *all* okay.'

The stunted pine declares from someone's backyard
you happen to be passing, 'I don't begrudge you
your good health. In fact, my blessing – you've got it, now.'

An ironing board is irrepressible.
'Your success is far from certain, my friend,
and still it's vital to my happiness.'

The yellow kernels in the dust, mere chicken feed,
call out, 'We salute you, and you can count on us.'

We do not live in a world of things
but among benedictions given
and – do you know what I'm saying? – received.

ADRIAN MITCHELL 1932–

STUFFERATION

Lovers lie around in it
Broken glass is found in it
Grass
I like that stuff

Tuna fish get trapped in it
Legs come wrapped in it
Nylon
I like that stuff

Eskimos and tramps chew it
Madame Tussaud gave status to it
Wax
I like that stuff

Elephants get sprayed with it
Scotch is made with it
Water
I like that stuff

Clergy are dumbfounded by it
Bones are surrounded by it
Flesh
I like that stuff

Harps are strung with it
Mattresses are sprung with it
Wire
I like that stuff

Carpenters make cots of it
Undertakers use lots of it
Wood
I like that stuff

Cigarettes are lit by it
Pensioners get happy when they sit by it
Fire
I like that stuff

Dankworth's alto is made of it, most of it,
Scoobdidoo is composed of it
Plastic
I like that stuff

Apemen take it to make them hairier
I ate a ton of it in Bulgaria
Yoghurt
I like that stuff

Man-made fibres and raw materials
Old rolled gold and breakfast cereals
Platinum linoleum
I like that stuff

Skin on my hands
Hair on my head
Toenails on my feet
And linen on the bed

Well I like that stuff
Yes I like that stuff
The earth
Is made of earth
And I like that stuff

KATHLEEN JAMIE 1962–

THE WAY WE LIVE

Pass the tambourine, let me bash out praises
to the Lord God of movement, to Absolute
non-friction, flight, and the scarey side:
death by avalanche, birth by failed contraception.
Of chicken tandoori and reggae, loud, from tenements,
commitment, driving fast and unswerving
friendship. Of tee-shirts on pulleys, giros and Bombay,
barmen, dreaming waitresses with many fake-gold
bangles. Of airports, impulse, and waking to uncertainty,
to strip-lights, motorways, or that pantheon –
the mountains. To overdrafts and grafting

and the fit slow pulse of wipers as you're
creeping over Rannoch, while the God of moorland
walks abroad with his entourage of freezing fog,
his bodyguard of snow.
Of endless gloaming in the North, of Asiatic swelter,
to launderettes, anecdotes, passions and exhaustion,
Final Demands and dead men, the skeletal grip
of government. To misery and elation; mixed,
the sod and caprice of landlords.
To the way it fits, the way it is, the way it seems
to be: let me bash out praises – pass the tambourine.

GABRIEL CELAYA 1911–91

GREAT MOMENTS
translated by ROBERT MEZEY

When it rains, and I go over my papers and end up
throwing everything into the fire: unfinished poems,
bills still unpaid, letters from dead friends,
photographs, kisses preserved in a book,
I am throwing off the dead weight of my hard-headed past,
I am shining and growing just as fast as I disown myself,
so if I poke at the fire, leap over the flames,
and scarcely understand what I feel while I'm doing it,
is it not happiness that is lifting me up?

When I hit the streets, whistling in sheer delight
– a cigarette in my lips, my soul in good order –
and I talk to the kids or let myself drift with the clouds,
early May and the breeze goes lifting up everything,
the young girls begin wearing their low-cut blouses, their arms
naked and tanned, their eyes wide,
and they laugh without knowing why, bubbling over
and scattering their ecstasy which then trembles afresh,
isn't it happiness, what we feel then?

When a friend shows up and there's nothing in the house,
But my girl brings forth anchovies, ham, and cheese,
olives and crab and two bottles of white wine,
and I assist at the miracle – knowing it's all on credit –
and I don't want to worry about having to pay for it,
and we drink and babble like there's no tomorrow,
and my friend is well off and he figures we are too,
and maybe we are, laughing at death that way,
isn't that happiness which suddenly breaks through?

When I wake up, I stay stretched out
by the open balcony. And dawn comes: the birds
trill sweetly in their heathen arabics;
and I ought to get up, but I don't;
and looking up I watch the rippling light of the sea
dancing on the ceiling, prism of its mother-of-pearl,
and I go on lying there and nothing matters a damn –
don't I annihilate time? And save myself from terror?
Isn't it happiness that comes with the dawn?

When I go to the market, I look at the nectarines
and work my jaws at the sight of the plump cherries,
the oozing figs, the plums fallen
from the tree of life, a sin no doubt,
being so tempting and all. And I ask the price
and haggle over it and finally knock it down,
but the game is over, I pay double and it's still not much,
and the salesgirl turns her astonished eyes on me,
is it not happiness that is germinating there?

When I can say: The day is over.
And by day I mean its taxis, its business,
the scrambling for money, the struggles of the dead.
And when I get home, sweat-stained and tired,
I sit down in the dusk and plug the phonograph in
and Kachaturian comes on, or Mozart, or Vivaldi,
and the music holds sway, I feel clean again,
simply clean and, in spite of everything, unhurt,
is it not happiness that is closing around me?

When after turning things over and over again in my mind,
I remember a friend and go over to see him, he says
'I was just now thinking of going over to see you.'
And we talk a long time, not about my troubles,
and he couldn't help me, even if he wanted to,
but we talk about how things are going in Jordan,
or a book of Neruda's, or his tailor, or the wind,
and as I leave I feel comforted and full of peace,
isn't that happiness, what comes over me then?

Opening a window; feeling the cool air;
walking down a road that smells of honeysuckle;
drinking with a friend; chattering or, better yet, keeping still;
feeling that we feel what other men feel;
seeing ourselves through eyes that see us as innocent,
isn't this happiness, and the hell with death?
Beaten, betrayed, seeing almost cynically
that they can do no more to me, that I'm still alive,
isn't this happiness, that is not for sale?

TACHIBANA AKEMI 1812–68

POEMS OF SOLITARY DELIGHTS
translated by GEOFFREY BOWNAS and ANTHONY THWAITE

What a delight it is
When on the bamboo matting
In my grass-thatched hut,
All on my own,
I make myself at ease.

What a delight it is
When, borrowing
Rare writings from a friend,
I open out
The first sheet.

What a delight it is
When, spreading paper,
I take my brush
And find my hand
Better than I thought.

What a delight it is
When, after a hundred days
Of racking my brains,
That verse that wouldn't come
Suddenly turns out well.

What a delight it is
When, of a morning,
I get up and go out
To find in full bloom a flower
That yesterday was not there.

What a delight it is
When, skimming through the pages
Of a book, I discover
A man written of there
Who is just like me.

What a delight it is
When everyone admits
It's a very difficult book,
And I understand it
With no trouble at all.

What a delight it is
When I blow away the ash,
To watch the crimson
Of the glowing fire
And hear the water boil.

What a delight it is
When a guest you cannot stand
Arrives, then says to you
'I'm afraid I can't stay long,'
And soon goes home.

What a delight it is
When I find a good brush,
Steep it hard in water,
Lick it on my tongue
And give it its first try.

FLEUR ADCOCK 1934–

LONDONER

Scarcely two hours back in the country
and I'm shopping in East Finchley High Road
in a cotton skirt, a cardigan, jandals –
or flipflops as people call them here,
where February's winter. Aren't I cold?
The neighbours in their overcoats are smiling
at my smiles and not at my bare toes:
they know me here.
                 I hardly know myself,
yet. It takes me until Monday evening,
walking from the office after dark
to Westminster Bridge. It's cold, it's foggy,
the traffic's as abominable as ever,
and there across the Thames is County Hall,
that uninspired stone body, floodlit.
It makes me laugh. In fact, it makes me sing.

'My babe so beautiful! it thrills my heart
With tender gladness, thus to look at thee'

from 'Frost at Midnight'

PERCY BYSSHE SHELLEY 1792–1822

TO IANTHE

I love thee, Baby! For thine own sweet sake;
  Those azure eyes, that faintly dimpled cheek.
  Thy tender frame, so eloquently weak,
  Love in the sternest heart of hate might wake;
But more when o'er thy fitful slumber bending
  Thy mother folds thee to her wakeful heart,
  Whilst love and pity, in her glances bending,
  All that thy passive eyes can feel impart:
More, when some feeble lineaments of her,
  Who bore thy weight beneath her spotless bosom,
  As with deep love I read thy face, recur! –
More dear art thou, O fair and fragile blossom;
  Dearest when most thy tender traits express
  The image of thy mother's loveliness.

ANNE RIDLER 1912–

INVOCATION from FOR A CHRISTENING

Blessing, sleep and grow taller in sleeping.
Lie ever in kind keeping.
Infants curl in a cowrie of peace
And should lie lazy. After this ease,
When the soul out of its safe shell goes,
Stretched as you stretch those knees and toes,
What should I wish you? Intelligence first,
In a credulous age by instruction cursed.
Take from us both what immunity
We have from the germ of the printed lie.
Your father's calm temper I wish you, and
The shaping power of his confident hand.
Much, too, that is different and your own;
And may we learn to leave you alone.
For your part, forgive us the pain of living,
Grow in that harsh sun great-hearted and loving.
Sleep, little honey, then; sleep while the powers
Of the Nine Bright Shiners and the Seven Stars
Harmless, encircle: the natural world
Lifegiving, neutral, unless despoiled
By our greed or scorn. And wherever you sleep –
My arms outgrown – or waking weep,
Life is your lot: you lie in God's hand,
In his terrible mercy, world without end.

JENI COUZYN 1942–

TRANSFORMATION

I see you dart into the world
pearly pink like the inside of a shell
streaked with silver.

Look! Look!
I am shouting with joy, rising up
like a phoenix from my pain

With my eyes I behold you
In the flesh I behold you

So a holy man waking into death
from a life of devotion or
martyrdom in flames

might look into the shining face of god
and see at once
he had never believed.

I see you with my eyes
I see you in glory.

From a tatter of flesh I watch them work.
From a pinnacle of joy.
The placenta, purplish liver meat

sails out of my body like a whale
rubbery hands turn it inside out
hold it up to the light.

The sinewy pulsing cord.
In a haze of peace they cut and stitch
my threaded body like scarlet linen

the midwife chatting comfortably
seated at her work, the needle threaded,
the thimble, the green thread

in and out, in and out.
Then washed and trim in clean sheets
they leave us: mother father child

three folded together.
I see your sleeping face
eyelids crescent lines, lips curled translucent

in stillness like a cowrie shell
whirlpool of your hair. I see you breathe.
In a still pool the moon lies quiet.

SAMUEL TAYLOR COLERIDGE 1772–1834

FROST AT MIDNIGHT

The Frost performs its secret ministry,
Unhelped by any wind. The owlet's cry
Came loud—and hark, again! loud as before.
The inmates of my cottage, all at rest,
Have left me to that solitude, which suits
Abstruser musings: save that at my side
My cradled infant slumbers peacefully.
'Tis calm indeed! so calm, that it disturbs
And vexes meditation with its strange
And extreme silentness. Sea, hill, and wood,
This populous village! Sea, and hill, and wood,
With all the numberless goings-on of life,
Inaudible as dreams! the thin blue flame
Lies on my low-burnt fire, and quivers not;
Only that film, which fluttered on the grate,
Still flutters there, the sole unquiet thing.
Methinks its motion in this hush of nature
Gives it dim sympathies with me who live,
Making it a companionable form,
Whose puny flaps and freaks the idling Spirit
By its own moods interprets, everywhere
Echo or mirror seeking of itself,
And makes a toy of Thought.

But O! how oft,
How oft, at school, with most believing mind,
Presageful, have I gazed upon the bars,
To watch that fluttering *stranger!* and as oft
With unclosed lids, already had I dreamt
Of my sweet birthplace, and the old church tower,
Whose bells, the poor man's only music, rang
From morn to evening, all the hot Fair-day,
So sweetly, that they stirred and haunted me
With a wild pleasure, falling on mine ear

Most like articulate sounds of things to come!
So gazed I, till the soothing things, I dreamt,
Lulled me to sleep, and sleep prolonged my dreams!
And so I brooded all the following morn,
Awed by the stern preceptor's face, mine eye
Fixed with mock study on my swimming book:
Save if the door half opened, and I snatched
A hasty glance, and still my heart leaped up,
For still I hoped to see the *stranger's* face,
Townsman, or aunt, or sister more beloved,
My playmate when we both were clothed alike!

Dear Babe, that sleepest cradled by my side,
Whose gentle breathings, heard in this deep calm,
Fill up the interspersèd vacancies
And momentary pauses of the thought!
My babe so beautiful! it thrills my heart
With tender gladness, thus to look at thee,
And think that thou shalt learn far other lore,
And in far other scenes! For I was reared
In the great city, pent 'mid cloisters dim,
And saw nought lovely but the sky and stars.
But *thou*, my babe! shalt wander like a breeze
By lakes and sandy shores, beneath the crags
Of ancient mountain, and beneath the clouds,
Which image in their bulk both lakes and shores
And mountain crags: so shalt thou see and hear
The lovely shapes and sounds intelligible
Of that eternal language, which thy God
Utters, who from eternity doth teach
Himself in all, and all things in himself.
Great universal Teacher! he shall mold
Thy spirit, and by giving make it ask.

Therefore all seasons shall be sweet to thee,
Whether the summer clothe the general earth
With greenness, or the redbreast sit and sing
Betwixt the tufts of snow on the bare branch
Of mossy apple tree, while the nigh thatch
Smokes in the sun-thaw; whether the eave-drops fall
Heard only in the trances of the blast,
Or if the secret ministry of frost
Shall hang them up in silent icicles,
Quietly shining to the quiet Moon.

PENELOPE SHUTTLE 1947–

DELICIOUS BABIES

Because of spring there are babies everywhere,
sweet or sulky, irascible or full of the milk of human
    kindness.
Yum, yum! Delicious babies!
Babies with the soft skins of babies, cheeks
of such tit-bit pinkness, tickle-able babies, tasty babies,
mouth-watering babies.

The pads of their hands! The rounds
of their knees! Their good smells of bathtime
and new clothes and gobbled rusks!
Even their discarded nappies are worthy of them, reveal
    their powers.
Legions and hosts of babies! Babies bold as lions, sighing
    babies,
tricksy babies, omniscient babies, babies using a plain
    language
of reasonable demands and courteous acceptance.
Others have the habit of loud contradiction,
can empty a railway carriage (though their displeasing
    howls
cheer up childless women).
Look at this baby, sitting bolt upright in his buggy!
Consider his lofty unsmiling acknowledgement of our
    adulation.

Look at the elfin golfer's hat flattering his fluffy hair!
Look next at this very smallest of babies
tightly wrapped in a foppery of blankets.
In his high promenading pram he sleeps sumptuously,
only a nose, his father's, a white bonnet and a wink
of eyelid showing.

All babies are manic-serene, all babies are mine,
all babies are edible, the boys taste best.
I feed on them, nectareous are my babies,
manna, confiture, my sweet groceries.

I smack my lips,
deep in my belly the egg ripens,
makes the windows shake,
another ovum-quake
moves earth, sky and me...

Bring me more babies! Let me have them for breakfast,
lunch and tea! Let me feast, let my honey-banquet of babies
go on forever, fresh deliveries night and day!

AMBROSE PHILIPS 1674–1749

TO MISS CHARLOTTE PULTENEY
IN HER MOTHER'S ARMS

Timely blossom, infant fair,
Fondling of a happy pair,
Every morn and every night,
Their solicitous delight,
Sleeping, waking, still at ease,
Pleasing, without skill to please,
Little gossip, blithe and hale,
Tattling many a broken tale,
Singing many a tuneless song,
Lavish of a heedless tongue,
Simple maiden, void of art,
Babbling out the very heart,
Yet abandoned to thy will,
Yet imagining no ill,
Yet too innocent to blush,
Like the linlet in the bush,
To the mother-linnet's note
Moduling her slender throat,
Chirping forth thy petty joys,
Wanton in the change of toys,
Like the linnet green in May,
Flitting to each bloomy spray,
Wearied then, and glad of rest,
Like the linlet in the nest.
This thy present happy lot,
This, in time, will be forgot:
Other pleasures, other cares,
Ever-busy time prepares;
And thou shalt in thy daughter see
This picture, once, resembled thee.

ROBERT BURNS 1759–96

A POET'S WELCOME TO HIS LOVE-BEGOTTEN DAUGHTER; THE FIRST INSTANCE THAT ENTITLED HIM TO THE VENERABLE APPELLATION OF FATHER

Thou's welcome, wean! Mischanter fa' me,
If thoughts o' thee, or yet thy Mamie,
Shall ever daunton me or awe me,
    My bonie lady;
Or if I blush when thou shalt ca' me
    Tyta, or Daddie.

Though now they ca' me fornicator,
And tease my name in kintra clatter,
The mair they talk, I'm kend the better;
    E'en let them clash!
An auld wife's tongue's a feckless matter
    To gie ane fash.

Welcome! My bonie, sweet wee dochter!
Though ye come here a wee unsought for;
And though your comin I hae fought for,
    Baith Kirk and Queir;
Yet by my faith, ye're no unwrought for,
    That I shall swear!

Wee image o' my bonie Betty,
As fatherly I kiss and daut thee,
As dear and near my heart I set thee,
    Wi' as gude will,
As a' the Priests had seen me get thee
    That's out o' h—.

Sweet fruit o' monie a merry dint,
My funny toil is no a' tint;
Though ye come to the warld asklent,

Which fools may scoff at,
In my last plack your part's be in't,
  The better half o't.

Though I should be the waur bestead,
Thou's be as braw and bienly clad,
And thy young years as nicely bred
  Wi' education,
As any brat o' Wedlock's bed,
  In a' thy station.

Lord grant that thou may ay inherit
Thy Mither's looks an' gracefu' merit;
An' thy poor, worthless Daddie's spirit,
  Without his failins!
'Twad please me mair to see thee heir it
  Than stocked mailins!

For if thou be, what I wad hae thee,
And tak the counsel I shall gie thee,
I'll never rue my trouble wi' thee,
  The cost nor shame o't,
But be a loving Father to thee,
  And brag the name o't.

SYLVIA PLATH 1932–63

YOU'RE

Clownlike, happiest on your hands,
Feet to the stars, and moon-skulled,
Gilled like a fish. A common-sense
Thumbs-down on the dodo's mode.
Wrapped up in yourself like a spool,
Trawling your dark as owls do.
Mute as a turnip from the Fourth
Of July to All Fools' Day,
O high-riser, my little loaf.

Vague as fog and looked for like mail.
Farther off than Australia.
Bent-backed Atlas, our traveled prawn.
Snug as a bud and at home
Like a sprat in a pickle jug
A creel of eels, all ripples.
Jumpy as a Mexican bean.
Right, like a well-done sum.
A clean slate, with your own face on.

SHARON OLDS 1942–

THE MONTH OF JUNE: 13½

As my daughter approaches graduation and
puberty at the same time, at her
own calm deliberate serious rate,
she begins to kick up her heels, jazz out her
hands, thrust out her hip-bones, chant
I'm great! I'm great! She feels 8th grade coming
open around her, a chrysalis cracking and
letting her out, it falls behind her and
joins the other husks on the ground,
7th grade, 6th grade, the
purple rind of 5th grade, the
hard jacket of 4th when she had so much pain,
3rd grade, 2nd, the dim cocoon of
1st grade back there somewhere on the path, and
kindergarten like a strip of thumb-suck blanket
taken from the actual blanket they wrapped her in at birth.
The whole school is coming off her shoulders like a
cloak unclasped, and she dances forth in her
jerky sexy child's joke dance of
self, self, her throat tight and a
hard new song coming out of it, while her
two dark eyes shine
above her body like a good mother and a
good father who look down and
love everything their baby does, the way she
lives their love.

'Now that I am fifty-six
Come and celebrate with me—'

from 'Rondel'

THOMAS NASHE 1567–1601

SPRING, THE SWEET SPRING
from SUMMER'S LAST WILL

Spring, the sweet spring, is the year's pleasant king,
Then blooms each thing, then maids dance in a ring,
Cold doth not sting, the pretty birds do sing:
   Cuckoo, jug-jug, pu-we, to-witta-woo!

The palm and may make country houses gay,
Lambs frisk and play, the shepherds pipe all day,
And we hear aye birds tune this merry lay:
   Cuckoo, jug-jug, pu-we, to-witta-woo!

The fields breathe sweet, the daisies kiss our feet,
Young lovers meet, old wives a-sunning sit,
In every street these tunes our ears do greet:
   Cuckoo, jug-jug, pu-we, to-witta-woo!
      Spring, the sweet spring!

GEOFFREY CHAUCER 1343?–1400

ROUNDEL from THE PARLIAMENT OF FOWLS

Now welcome Summer with thy sunne soft,
That hast this winter's weathers overshake,
And driven away the longe nightes black.

Saint Valentine, that art full high aloft,
Thus singen smalle fowles for thy sake:
Now welcome Summer with thy sunne soft,
That hast this winter's weathers overshake.

Well have they cause for to gladden oft,
Since each of them recovered hath his make.
Full blissful may they singe when they wake:
Now welcome Summer with thy sunne soft,
That hast this winter's weather's overshake,
And driven away the longe nightes black!

JOHN KEATS 1795–1821

TO AUTUMN

Season of mists and mellow fruitfulness,
　Close bosom-friend of the maturing sun;
Conspiring with him how to load and bless
　With fruit the vines that round the thatch-eaves run;
To bend with apples the mossed cottage-trees,
　And fill all fruit with ripeness to the core;
　　To swell the gourd, and plump the hazel shells
　With a sweet kernel; to set budding more,
And still more, later flowers for the bees,
Until they think warm days will never cease,
　　For Summer has o'er-brimmed their clammy cells.

Who hath not seen thee oft amid thy store?
　Sometimes whoever seeks abroad may find
Thee sitting careless on a granary floor,
　Thy hair soft-lifted by the winnowing wind;
Or on a half-reaped furrow sound asleep.
　Drowsed with the fume of poppies, while thy hook
　　Spares the next swath and all its twinéd flowers:
And sometimes like a gleaner thou dost keep
　Steady thy laden head across a brook;
　Or by a cider-press, with patient look,
　　Thou watchest the last oozings hours by hours.

Where are the songs of Spring? Aye, where are they?
　Think not of them, thou hast thy music too—
While barréd clouds bloom the soft-dying day,
　And touch the stubble plains with rosy hue;
Then in a wailful choir the small gnats mourn
　Among the river sallows, borne aloft
　　Or sinking as the light wind lives or dies;
And full-grown lambs loud bleat from hilly bourn;
　Hedge crickets sing; and now with treble soft
　The redbreast whistles from a garden-croft;
　　And gathering swallows twitter in the skies.

DYLAN THOMAS 1914–53

POEM IN OCTOBER

It was my thirtieth year to heaven
Woke to my hearing from harbour and neighbour wood
And the mussel pooled and the heron
Priested shore
The morning beckon
With water praying and call of seagull and rook
And the knock of sailing boats on the net webbed wall
Myself to set foot
That second
In the still sleeping town and set forth.

My birthday began with the water-
birds and the birds of the winged trees flying my name
Above the farms and the white horses
And I rose
In rainy autumn
And walked abroad in a shower of all my days.
High tide and the heron dived when I took the road
Over the border
And the gates
Of the town closed as the town awoke.

A springful of larks in a rolling
Cloud and the roadside bushes brimming with whistling
Blackbirds and the sun of October
Summery
On the hill's shoulder,
Here were fond climates and sweet singers suddenly
Come in the morning where I wandered and listened
To the rain wringing
Wind blow cold
In the wood faraway under me.

Pale rain over the dwindling harbour
And over the sea wet church the size of a snail

With its horns through mist and the castle
Brown as owls
But all the gardens
Of spring and summer were blooming in the tall tales
Beyond the border and under the lark full cloud.
There could I marvel
My birthday
Away but the weather turned around.

It turned away from the blithe country
And down the other air and the blue altered sky
Streamed again a wonder of summer
With apples
Pears and red currants
And I saw in the turning so clearly a child's
Forgotten mornings when he walked with his mother
Through the parables
Of sun light
And the legends of the green chapels

And the twice told fields of infancy
That his tears burned my cheeks and his heart moved in mine.
These were the woods the river and sea
Where a boy
In the listening
Summertime of the dead whispered the truth of his joy
To the trees and the stones and the fish in the tide.
And the mystery
Sang alive
Still in the water and singingbirds.

And there could I marvel my birthday
Away but the weather turned around. And the true
Joy of the long dead child sang burning

In the sun.
It was my thirtieth
Year to heaven stood there then in the summer noon
Though the town below lay leaved with October blood.
O may my heart's truth
Still be sung
On this high hill in a year's turning.

JONATHAN SWIFT 1667–1745

ON STELLA'S BIRTHDAY, 1719

Stella this day is thirty-four,
(We shan't dispute a year or more:)
However Stella, be not troubled,
Although thy size and years are doubled,
Since first I saw thee at sixteen,
The brightest virgin on the green;
So little is thy form declin'd;
Made up so largely in thy mind.

   Oh, would it please the gods to *split*
Thy beauty, size, and years, and wit,
No age could furnish out a pair
Of nymphs so graceful, wise and fair;
With half the lustre of your eyes,
With half your wit, your years, and size.
And then before it grew too late,
How should I beg of gentle Fate,
(That either nymph might have her swain,)
To split my worship too in twain.

WALT WHITMAN 1819–92

from SONG OF MYSELF

I celebrate myself, and sing myself,
And what I assume you shall assume,
For every atom belonging to me as good belongs to you.

I loafe and invite my soul,
I lean and loafe at my ease observing a spear of summer grass.

My tongue, every atom of my blood, form'd from this soil, this air,
Born here of parents born here from parents the same, and their
    parents the same,
I, now thirty-seven years old in perfect health begin,
Hoping to cease not till death.

ELAINE FEINSTEIN 1930–

GETTING OLDER

The first surprise: I like it.
Whatever happens now, some things
that used to terrify have not:

I didn't die young, for instance. Or lose
my only love. My three children
never had to run away from anyone.

Don't tell me this gratitude is complacent.
We all approach the edge of the same blackness
which for me is silent.

Knowing as much sharpens
my delight in January freesia,
hot coffee, winter sunlight. So we say

as we lie close on some gentle occasion:
every day won from such
darkness is a celebration.

ROGER MCGOUGH 1937–

A JOY TO BE OLD

It's a joy to be old.
Kids through school,
The dog dead and the car sold.

Worth their weight in gold,
Bus passes. Let asses rule.
It's a joy to be old.

The library when it's cold.
Immune from ridicule.
The dog dead and the car sold.

Time now to be bold.
Skinnydipping in the pool.
It's a joy to be old.

Death cannot be cajoled.
No rewinding the spool.
The dog dead and the car sold.

Don't have your fortune told.
Have fun playing the fool.
It's a joy to be old.
The dog dead and the car sold.

MURIEL RUKEYSER 1913–80

RONDEL

Now that I am fifty-six
Come and celebrate with me—

What happens to song and sex
Now that I am fifty-six?

They dance, but differently,
Death and distance in the mix;
Now that I'm fifty-six
Come and celebrate with me.

JENNY JOSEPH 1932–

WARNING

When I am an old woman I shall wear purple
With a red hat which doesn't go, and doesn't suit me.
And I shall spend my pension on brandy and summer gloves
And satin sandals, and say we've no money for butter.
I shall sit down on the pavement when I'm tired
And gobble up samples in shops and press alarm bells
And run my stick along the public railings
And make up for the sobriety of my youth.
I shall go out in my slippers in the rain
And pick the flowers in other people's gardens
And learn to spit.

You can wear terrible shirts and grow more fat
And eat three pounds of sausages at a go
Or only bread and pickle for a week
And hoard pens and pencils and beermats and things in boxes.

But now we must have clothes that keep us dry
And pay our rent and not swear in the street
And set a good example for the children.
We must have friends to dinner and read the papers.

But maybe I ought to practise a little now?
So people who know me are not too shocked and surprised
When suddenly I am old, and start to wear purple.

ROGER MCGOUGH 1937–

SCINTILLATE

I have outlived
my youthfulness
So a quiet life for me.

Where once
I used to
scintillate

now I sin
till ten
past three.

PERCY BYSSHE SHELLEY 1792–1822

from ADONAIS, AN ELEGY ON THE DEATH OF JOHN KEATS

Peace, peace! he is not dead, he doth not sleep –
He hath awakened from the dream of life –
'Tis we, who lost in stormy visions, keep
With phantoms an unprofitable strife,
And in mad trance, strike with our spirit's knife
Invulnerable nothings. – *We* decay
Like corpses in a charnel; fear and grief
Convulse us and consume us day by day,
And cold hopes swarm like worms within our living clay.

He has outsoared the shadow of our night;
Envy and calumny and hate and pain,
And that unrest which men miscall delight,
Can touch him not and torture not again;
From the contagion of the world's slow stain
He is secure, and now can never mourn
A heart grown cold, a head grown gray in vain;
Nor, when the spirit's self has ceased to burn,
With sparkless ashes load an unlamented urn.

He lives, he wakes – 'tis Death is dead, not he;
Mourn not for Adonais. – Thou young Dawn,
Turn all thy dew to splendour, for from thee
The spirit thou lamentest is not gone;
Ye caverns and ye forests, cease to moan!
Cease, ye faint flowers and fountains, and thou Air,
Which like a mourning veil thy scarf hadst thrown
O'er the abandoned Earth, now leave it bare
Even to the joyous stars which smile on its despair!

He is made one with Nature: there is heard
His voice in all her music, from the moan
Of thunder, to the song of night's sweet bird;

He is a presence to be felt and known
In darkness and in light, from herb and stone,
Spreading itself where'er that Power may move
Which has withdrawn his being to its own;
Which wields the world with never-wearied love,
Sustains it from beneath, and kindles it above.

He is a portion of the loveliness
Which once he made more lovely: he doth bear
His part, while the one Spirit's plastic stress
Sweeps through the dull dense world, compelling there
All new successions to the forms they wear;
Torturing th' unwilling dross that checks its flight
To its own likeness, as each mass may bear;
And bursting in its beauty and its might
From trees and beasts and men into the Heaven's light.

ANNA AKHMATOVA 1889–1966

from REQUIEM: POEMS 1935–1940
translated by RICHARD MCKANE

The hour of remembrance has drawn close again.
I see you, hear you, feel you:

the one they could hardly get to the window,
the one who no longer walks on this earth,

the one who shook her beautiful head,
and said: 'Coming here is like coming home.'

I would like to name them all but they took away
the list and there's no way of finding them.

For them I have woven a wide shroud
from the humble words I heard among them.

I remember them always, everywhere,
I will never forget them, whatever comes.

'Because I love'

from 'Amo Ergo Sum'

KATHLEEN RAINE 1908–

AMO ERGO SUM

Because I love
    The sun pours out its rays of living gold
    Pours out its gold and silver on the sea.

Because I love
    The earth upon her astral spindle winds
    Her ecstasy-producing dance.

Because I love
    Clouds travel on the winds through wide skies,
    Skies wide and beautiful, blue and deep.

Because I love
    Wind blows white sails,
    The wind blows over flowers, the sweet wind blows.

Because I love
    The ferns grown green, and green the grass, and green
    The transparent sunlit trees.

Because I love
    Larks rise up from the grass
    And all the leaves are full of singing birds.

Because I love
    The summer air quivers with a thousand wings,
    Myriads of jewelled eyes burn in the light.

Because I love
    The iridescent shells upon the sand
    Take forms as fine and intricate as thought.

Because I love
    There is an invisible way across the sky,

Birds travel by that way, the sun and moon
And all the stars travel that path by night.

Because I love
There is a river flowing all night long.

Because I love
All night the river flows into my sleep,
Ten thousand living things are sleeping in my arms,
And sleeping wake, and flowing are at rest.

JENNY JOSEPH 1932–

THE SUN HAS BURST THE SKY

The sun has burst the sky
Because I love you
And the river its banks.

The sea laps the great rocks
Because I love you
And takes no heed of the moon dragging it away
And saying coldly 'Constancy is not for you'.

The blackbird fills the air
Because I love you
With spring and lawns and shadows falling on lawns.

The people walk in the street and laugh
I love you
And far down the river ships sound their hooters
Crazy with joy because I love you.

ADRIAN HENRI 1932–2000

LOVE IS ...

Love is feeling cold in the back of vans
Love is a fanclub with only two fans
Love is walking holding paintstained hands
Love is

Love is fish and chips on winter nights
Love is blankets full of strange delights
Love is when you don't put out the light
Love is

Love is the presents in Christmas shops
Love is when you're feeling Top of the Pops
Love is what happens when the music stops
Love is

Love is white panties lying all forlorn
Love is a pink nightdress still slightly warm
Love is when you have to leave at dawn
Love is

Love is you and love is me
Love is a prison and love is free
Love's what's there when you're away from me
Love is ...

CHRISTINA ROSSETTI 1830–94

A BIRTHDAY

My heart is like a singing bird
   Whose nest is in a watered shoot;
My heart is like an apple-tree
   Whose boughs are bent with thickset fruit;
My heart is like a rainbow shell
   That paddles in a halcyon sea;
My heart is gladder than all these
   Because my love is come to me.

Raise me a dais of silk and down;
   Hang it with vair and purple dyes;
Carve it in doves and pomegranates,
   And peacocks with a hundred eyes;
Work it in gold and silver grapes,
   In leaves and silver fleurs-de-lys;
Because the birthday of my life
   Is come, my love is come to me.

SIR PHILIP SIDNEY 1554–86

'MY TRUE LOVE HATH MY HEART AND I HAVE HIS'

My true love hath my heart and I have his,
By just exchange one for the other given.
I hold his dear, and mine he cannot miss,
There never was a better bargain driven.
    My true love hath my heart and I have his.

His heart in me keeps me and him in one,
My heart in him his thoughts and senses guides:
He loves my heart, for once it was his own,
I cherish his because in me it bides.
    My true love hath my heart, and I have his.

E.E. CUMMINGS 1894–1962

I CARRY YOUR HEART WITH ME

i carry your heart with me(i carry it in
my heart)i am never without it(anywhere
i go you go,my dear;and whatever is done
by only me is your doing,my darling)
                                        i fear
no fate(for you are my fate,my sweet)i want
no world(for beautiful you are my world,my true)
and it's you are whatever a moon has always meant
and whatever a sun will always sing is you

here is the deepest secret nobody knows
(here is the root of the root and the bud of the bud
and the sky of the sky of a tree called life;which grows
higher than soul can hope or mind can hide)
and this is the wonder that's keeping the stars apart

i carry your heart(i carry it in my heart)

WENDY COPE 1945–

AS SWEET

It's all because we're so alike –
Twin souls, we two.
We smile at the expression, yes,
And know it's true.

I told the shrink. He gave our love
A different name.
But he can call it what he likes –
It's still the same.

I long to see you, hear your voice,
My narcissistic object-choice.

JOHN DONNE 1572–1631

THE GOOD-MORROW

I wonder, by my troth, what thou and I
Did, till we loved? were we not weaned till then?
But sucked on country pleasures, childishly?
Or snorted we in the Seven Sleepers' den?
'Twas so; but this, all pleasures fancies be.
If ever any beauty I did see,
Which I desired, and got, 'twas but a dream of thee.

And now good-morrow to our waking souls,
Which watch not one another out of fear;
For love, all love of other sights controls,
And makes one little room an everywhere.
Let sea-discoverers to new worlds have gone,
Let maps to others, worlds on worlds have shown,
Let us possess one world, each hath one, and is one.

My face in thine eye, thine in mine appears,
And true plain hearts do in the faces rest;
Where can we find two better hemispheres,
Without sharp North, without declining West?
Whatever dies was not mixed equally;
If our two loves be one, or, thou and I
Love so alike that none do slacken, none can die.

THOMAS HOOD 1799–1845

I LOVE THEE

I love thee – I love thee!
   'Tis all that I can say;
It is my vision in the night,
   My dreaming in the day;
The very echo of my heart,
   The blessing when I pray,
I love thee – I love thee,
   Is all that I can say.

I love thee – I love thee!
   Is ever on my tongue;
In all my proudest poesy
   That chorus still is sung;
It is the verdict of my eyes,
   Amidst the gay and young:
I love thee – I love thee,
   A thousand maids among.

I love thee – I love thee!
   Thy bright and hazel glance,
The mellow lute upon those lips,
   Whose tender tones entrance;
But most, dear heart of hearts, thy proofs
   That still these words enhance,
I love thee – I love thee;
   Whatever be thy chance.

ANNE BRADSTREET 1612–72

TO MY DEAR AND LOVING HUSBAND

If ever two were one, then surely we.
If ever man were loved by wife, then thee;
If ever wife was happy in a man,
Compare with me ye women if you can.
I prize thy love more than whole mines of gold,
Or all the riches that the East doth hold.
My love is such that rivers cannot quench,
Nor ought but love from thee give recompense.
Thy love is such I can no way repay;
The heavens reward thee manifold, I pray.
Then while we live, in love let's so persever,
That when we live no more, we may live ever.

WILLIAM SHAKESPEARE 1564–1616

SONNET 116

Let me not to the marriage of true minds
Admit impediments. Love is not love
Which alters when it alteration finds,
Or bends with the remover to remove:
Oh, no! it is an ever fixèd mark,
That looks on tempests and is never shaken;
It is the star to every wandering bark,
Whose worth's unknown, although his height be taken.
Love's not Time's fool, though rosy lips and cheeks
Within his bending sickle's compass come;
Love alters not with his brief hours and weeks,
But bears it out even to the edge of doom.
 If this be error and upon me proved,
 I never writ, nor no man ever loved.

ROBERT BURNS 1759–96

JOHN ANDERSON MY JO

John Anderson my jo, John,
   When we were first acquent;
Your locks were like the raven,
   Your bony brow was brent;
But now your brow is beld, John,
   Your locks are like the snaw;
But blessings on your frosty pow,
   John Anderson my jo.

John Anderson my jo, John,
   We clamb the hill the gither;
And mony a canty day, John,
   We've had wi' ane anither:
Now we maun totter down, John,
   And hand in hand we'll go;
And sleep the gither at the foot,
   John Anderson my jo.

CHRISTOPHER MARLOWE 1564–93

THE PASSIONATE SHEPHERD TO HIS LOVE

Come live with me and be my Love,
And we will all the pleasures prove
That valleys, groves, hills, and fields,
Woods, or steepy mountains yields.

And we will sit upon the rocks
Seeing the shepherds feed their flocks,
By shallow rivers, to whose falls
Melodious birds sing madrigals.

And I will make thee beds of roses
And a thousand fragrant posies,
A cap of flowers, and a kirtle
Embroidered all with leaves of myrtle;

A gown made of the finest wool,
Which from our pretty lambs we pull;
Fair linèd slippers for the cold,
With buckles of the purest gold;

A belt of straw and ivy buds
With coral clasps and amber studs;
And if these pleasures may thee move,
Come live with me and be my Love.

The shepherd swains shall dance and sing
For thy delight each May morning:
If these delights thy mind may move,
Then live with me and be my Love.

LANGSTON HUGHES 1902–67

HARLEM NIGHT SONG

Come,
Let us roam the night together
Singing.

I love you.

Across
The Harlem roof-tops
Moon is shining.
Night sky is blue.
Stars are great drops
Of golden dew.

Down the street
A band is playing.

I love you.

Come,
Let us roam the night together
Singing.

ALICE OSWALD 1966–

WEDDING

From time to time our love is like a sail
and when the sail begins to alternate
from tack to tack, it's like a swallowtail
and when the swallow flies it's like a coat;
and if the coat is yours, it has a tear
like a wide mouth and when the mouth begins
to draw the wind, it's like a trumpeter
and when the trumpet blows, it blows like millions...
and this, my love, is when millions come and go
beyond the need of us, is like a trick;
and when the trick begins, it's like a toe
tip-toeing on a rope, which is like luck;
and when the luck begins, it's like a wedding,
which is like love, which is like everything.

EDWIN MUIR 1887–1959

THE CONFIRMATION

Yes, yours, my love, is the right human face.
I in my mind had waited for this long,
Seeing the false and searching for the true,
Then found you as a traveller finds a place
Of welcome suddenly amid the wrong
Valleys and rocks and twisting roads. But you,
What shall I call you? A fountain in a waste,
A well of water in a country dry,
Or anything that's honest and good, an eye
That makes the whole world bright. Your open heart,
Simple with giving, gives the primal deed,
The first good world, the blossom, the blowing seed,
The hearth, the steadfast land, the wandering sea,
Not beautiful or rare in every part,
But like yourself, as they were meant to be.

JOHN KEATS 1795–1821

BRIGHT STAR

Bright Star! would I were steadfast as thou art –
Not in lone splendour hung aloft the night,
And watching, with eternal lids apart,
Like Nature's patient sleepless Eremite,
The moving waters at their priestlike task
Of pure ablution round earth's human shores,
Or gazing on the new soft fallen mask
Of snow upon the mountains and the moors –
No – yet still steadfast, still unchangeable,
Pillow'd upon my fair love's ripening breast
To feel for ever its soft fall and swell,
Awake for ever in a sweet unrest;
  Still, still to hear her tender-taken breath,
  And so live ever – or else swoon to death.

WILLIAM SHAKESPEARE 1564–1616

SONNET 18

Shall I compare thee to a summer's day?
Thou art more lovely and more temperate:
Rough winds do shake the darling buds of May,
And summer's lease hath all too short a date:
Sometime too hot the eye of heaven shines,
And often is his gold complexion dimm'd,
And every fair from fair sometime declines,
By chance or natures changing course untrimm'd:
But thy eternal summer shall not fade,
Nor lose possession of that fair thou owest,
Nor shall death brag thou wandrest in his shade,
When in eternal lines to time thou growest,
  So long as men can breathe or eyes can see
  So long lives this, and this gives life to thee.

ROBERT BURNS 1759–96

A RED, RED ROSE

O my luve's like a red, red rose,
　　That's newly sprung in June;
O my luve's like the melodie
　　That's sweetly played in tune.

As fair art thou, my bonnie lass,
　　So deep in luve am I;
And I will luve thee still, my dear,
　　Till a' the seas gang dry.

Till a' the seas gang dry, my dear,
　　And the rocks melt wi' the sun:
O I will love thee still, my dear,
　　While the sands o' life shall run.

And fare thee weel, my only luve,
　　And fare thee weel awhile!
And I will come again, my luve,
　　Though it were ten thousand mile.

SAMUEL TAYLOR COLERIDGE 1772–1834

LINES FROM A NOTEBOOK – FEBRUARY 1807

And in Life's noisiest hour,
There whispers still the ceaseless Love of Thee,
The heart's *Self-solace*, and soliloquy.

You mould my Hopes, you fashion me within;
And to the leading Love-throb in the Heart
Thro' all my being all my pulses beat.
You lie in all my many Thoughts, like Light
Like the fair Light of Dawn, or summer-Eve
On rippling Stream, or cloud-reflecting Lake.

And looking to the Heaven, that bends above you
How oft I bless the Lot, that made me love you.

CHRISTOPHER BRENNAN 1870-1932

BECAUSE SHE WOULD ASK ME WHY
I LOVED HER

If questioning could make us wise
no eyes would ever gaze in eyes;
if all our tale were told in speech
no mouths would wander each to each.

Were spirits free from mortal mesh
and love not bound in hearts of flesh
no aching breasts would yearn to meet
and find their ecstasy complete.

For who is there that lives and knows
the secret powers by which he grows?
were knowledge all, what were our need
to thrill and faint and sweetly bleed?

Then seek not, sweet, the *If* and *Why*
I love you now until I die:
For I must love because I live
And life in me is what you give.

ELIZABETH BARRETT BROWNING 1806–61

SONNET FROM THE PORTUGUESE XLIII

How do I love thee? Let me count the ways.
I love thee to the depth and breadth and height
My soul can reach, when feeling out of sight
For the ends of Being and ideal Grace.
I love thee to the level of everyday's
Most quiet need, by sun and candle-light.
I love thee freely, as men strive for Right;
I love thee purely, as they turn from Praise.
I love thee with the passion put to use
In my old griefs, and with my childhood's faith.
I love thee with a love I seemed to lose
With my lost saints—I love thee with the breath,
Smiles, tears, of all my life!—and, if God choose,
I shall but love thee better after death.

WENDY COPE 1945–

MY LOVER

For I will consider my lover, who shall remain nameless.

For at the age of 49 he can make the noise of five different kinds of lorry changing gear on a hill.

For he sometimes does this on the stairs at his place of work.

For he is embarrassed when people overhear him.

For he can also imitate at least three different kinds of train.

For these include the London tube train, the steam engine, and the Southern Rail electric.

For he supports Tottenham Hotspur with joyful and unswerving devotion.

For he abhors Arsenal, whose supporters are uncivilized and rough.

For he explains that Spurs are magic, whereas Arsenal are boring and defensive.

For I knew nothing of this six months ago, nor did I want to.

For now it all enchants me.

For this he performs in ten degrees.

For first he presents himself as a nice, serious, liberated person.

For secondly he sits through many lunches, discussing life and love and never mentioning football.

For thirdly he is careful not to reveal how much he dislikes losing an argument.

For fourthly he talks about the women in his past, acknowledging that some of it must have been his fault.

For fifthly he is so obviously reasonable that you are inclined to doubt this.

For sixthly he invites himself round for a drink one evening.

For seventhly you consume two bottles of wine between you.

For eighthly he stays the night.

For ninthly you cannot wait to see him again.
For tenthly he does not get in touch for several days.
For having achieved his object he turns again to his other
  interests.
For he will not miss his evening class or his choir practice
  for a woman.
For he is out nearly all the time.
For you cannot even get him on the telephone.
For he is the kind of man who has been driving women
  round the bend for generations.
For, sad to say, this does not bring you to your
  senses.
For he is charming.
For he is good with animals and children.
For his voice is both reassuring and sexy.
For he drives an A-registration Vauxhall Astra estate.
For he goes at 80 miles per hour on the motorways.
For when I plead with him he says, 'I'm not going any
  slower than *this*.'
For he is convinced he knows his way around better than
  anyone else on earth.
For he does not encourage suggestions from his
  passengers.
For if he ever got lost there would be hell to pay.
For he sometimes makes me sleep on the wrong side of my
  own bed.
For he cannot be bossed around.
For he has this grace, that he is happy to eat fish fingers or
  Chinese takeaway or to cook the supper himself.
For he knows about my cooking and is realistic.
For he makes me smooth cocoa with bubbles on the top.
For he drinks and smokes at least as much as I do.
For he is obsessed with sex.
For he would never say it is overrated.

For he grew up before the permissive society and
    remembers his adolescence.
For he does not insist it is healthy and natural, nor does he
    ask me what I would like him to do.
For he has a few ideas of his own.
For he has never been able to sleep much and talks with
    me late into the night.
For we wear each other out with our wakefulness.
For he makes me feel like a light-bulb that cannot switch
    itself off.
For he inspires poem after poem.
For he is clean and tidy but not too concerned with his
    appearance.
For he lets the barber cut his hair too short and goes
    round looking like a convict for a fortnight.
For when I ask if this necklace is all right he replies, 'Yes, if
    no means looking at three others.'
For he was shocked when younger team-mates began
    using talcum powder in the changing-room.
For his old-fashioned masculinity is the cause of continual
    merriment on my part.
For this puzzles him.

CHRISTOPHER MARLOWE 1564–93

THE FACE THAT LAUNCHED A THOUSAND SHIPS
from DOCTOR FAUSTUS

(Doctor Faustus speaks)

Was this the face that launched a thousand ships?
And burnt the topless towers of Ilium?
Sweet Helen, make me immortal with a kiss:
Her lips suck forth my soul, see where it flies!
Come Helen, come, give me my soul again.
Here will I dwell, for heaven is in these lips,
And all is dross that is not Helena.
I will be Paris, and for love of thee,
Instead of Troy shall Wertenberg be sack'd;
And I will combat with weak Menelaus,
And wear thy colours on my plumed crest;
Yea I will wound Achilles in the heel,
And then return to Helen for a kiss.
O thou art fairer than the evening air,
Clad in the beauty of a thousand stars:
Brighter art thou than flaming Jupiter,
When he appear'd to hapless Semele;
More lovely than the monarch of the sky
In wanton Arethusa's azur'd arms;
And none but thou shalt be my paramour.

BYRON, GEORGE GORDON, LORD 1788–1824

SHE WALKS IN BEAUTY

She walks in beauty, like the night
  Of cloudless climes and starry skies;
And all that's best of dark and bright
  Meet in her aspect and her eyes:
Thus mellowed to that tender light
  Which heaven to gaudy day denies.

One shade the more, one ray the less,
  Had half impaired the nameless grace
Which waves in every raven tress,
  Or softly lightens o'er her face;
Where thoughts serenely sweet express
  How pure, how dear their dwelling place.

And on that cheek, and o'er that brow,
  So soft, so calm, yet eloquent,
The smiles that win, the tints that glow,
  But tell of days in goodness spent,
A mind at peace with all below,
  A heart whose love is innocent!

EDMUND SPENSER 1552?–99

SONNET from AMORETTI

Oft when my spirit doth spread her bolder wings,
    In mind to mount up to the purest sky,
It down is weighed with thought of earthly things
    And clogged with burden of mortality,
    Where when that sovereign beauty it doth spy,
Resembling heaven's glory in her light,
    Drawn with sweet pleasure's bait, it back doth fly,
And unto heaven forgets her former flight.
There my frail fancy, fed with full delight,
    Doth bathe in bliss and mantleth most at ease:
Ne thinks of other heaven, but how it might
    Her heart's desire with most contentment please.
      Heart need not with none other happiness,
      But here on earth to have such heaven's bliss.

T.S. ELIOT 1885–1965

A DEDICATION TO MY WIFE

To whom I owe the leaping delight
That quickens my senses in our wakingtime
And the rhythm that governs the repose of our sleepingtime,
 The breathing in unison.

Of lovers whose bodies smell of each other
Who think the same thoughts without need of speech,
And babble the same speech without need of meaning.

No peevish winter wind shall chill
No sullen tropic sun shall wither
The roses in the rose-garden which is ours and ours only

But this dedication is for others to read:
These are private words addressed to you in public.

D.H. LAWRENCE 1885–1930

from FIDELITY

And man and woman are like the earth, that brings forth flowers
in summer, and love, but underneath is rock.
Older than flowers, older than ferns, older than foraminiferae
older than plasm altogether is the soul of a man underneath.
And when, throughout all the wild orgasms of love
slowly a gem forms, in the ancient, once-more-molten rocks
of two human hearts, two ancient rocks, a man's heart and a woman's,
that is the crystal of peace, the slow hard jewel of trust,
the sapphire of fidelity.
The gem of mutual peace emerging from the wild chaos of love.

'Such love I cannot analyse;
It does not rest in lips or eyes'

from 'Friendship'

STEVIE SMITH 1902–71

THE PLEASURES OF FRIENDSHIP

The pleasures of friendship are exquisite,
How pleasant to go to a friend on a visit!
I go to my friend, we walk on the grass,
And the hours and moments like minutes pass.

ELIZABETH JENNINGS 1926–

FRIENDSHIP

Such love I cannot analyse;
It does not rest in lips or eyes,
Neither in kisses nor caress.
Partly, I know, it's gentleness

And understanding in one word
Or in brief letters. It's preserved
By trust and by respect and awe.
These are the words I'm feeling for.

Two people, yes, two lasting friends.
The giving comes, the taking ends.
There is no measure for such things.
For this all Nature slows and sings.

COLE PORTER 1893–1964

FRIENDSHIP

If you're ever in a jam,
  Here I am.
If you're ever in a mess,
  S.O.S.
If you ever feel so happy you land in jail,
  I'm your bail.

It's friendship, friendship,
Just a perfect blendship.
When other friendships have been forgot,
Ours will still be hot.

If you're ever up a tree,
  Phone to me.
If you're ever down a well,
  Ring my bell.
If you ever lose your teeth and you're out to dine,
  Borrow mine.

It's friendship, friendship,
Just a perfect blendship.
When other friendships have been forgate,
Ours will still be great.

If they ever black your eyes,
  Put me wise.
If they ever cook your goose,
  Turn me loose.
If they ever put a bullet through your brain,
  I'll complain.

It's friendship, friendship,
Just a perfect blendship.
When other friendships have been forgit,
Ours will still be it.

EMILY BRONTË 1818–48

LOVE AND FRIENDSHIP

Love is like the wild rose-briar;
   Friendship like the holly-tree:
The holly is dark when the rose-briar blooms,
   But which will bloom most constantly?

The wild rose-briar is sweet in spring,
   Its summer blossoms scent the air;
Yet wait till winter comes again,
   And who will call the wild-briar fair?

Then, scorn the silly rose-wreath now,
   And deck thee with the holly's sheen,
That, when December blights thy brow,
   He still may leave thy garland green.

KATHERINE PHILIPS 1631–64

A RETIRED FRIENDSHIP, TO ARDELIA.
23 AUGUST 1651

Come, my Ardelia, to this bower
  Where, kindly mingling souls awhile,
Let's innocently spend an hour
  And at all serious follies smile.

Here is no quarrelling for crowns,
  Nor fear of changes in our fate,
No trembling at the great ones' frowns,
  Nor any slavery of state.

Here's no disguise, nor treachery,
  Nor any deep concealed design;
From blood and plots this place is free,
  And calm as are those looks of thine.

Here let us sit, and bless our stars
  Who did such happy quiet give,
As that removed from noise of wars
  In one another's hearts we live.

Why should we entertain a fear?
  Love cares not how the world is turned:
If crowds of dangers should appear,
  Yet friendship can be unconcerned.

We wear about us such a charm,
  No horror can be our offence,
For mischief's self can do no harm
  To friendship and to innocence.

Let's mark how soon Apollo's beams
  Command the flocks to quit their meat,
And not entreat the neighbour streams
  To quench their thirst, but cool their heat.

In such a scorching age as this,
  Whoever would not seek a shade
Deserve their happiness to miss,
  As having their own peace betrayed.

But we, of one another's mind
  Assured, the boisterous world disdain,
With quiet souls, and unconfined
  Enjoy what princes wish in vain.

JOHN MASEFIELD 1878–1967

BEING HER FRIEND

Being her friend, I do not care, not I,
  How gods or men may wrong me, beat me down;
Her word's sufficient star to travel by,
  I count her quiet praise sufficient crown.

Being her friend, I do not covet gold,
  Save for a royal gift to give her pleasure;
To sit with her, and have her hand to hold,
  Is wealth, I think, surpassing minted treasure.

Being her friend, I only covet art,
  A white pure flame to search me as I trace
In crooked letters from a throbbing heart,
  The hymn to beauty written on her face.

IVOR GURNEY 1890–1937

COMPANION – NORTH-EAST DUG-OUT

He talked of Africa,
    That fat and easy man.
I'd but to say a word,
    And straight the tales began.

And when I'd wish to read,
    That man would not disclose
A thought of harm, but sleep;
    Hard-breathing through his nose.

Then when I'd wish to hear
    More tales of Africa,
'Twas but to wake him up,
    And but a word to say

To press the button, and
    Keep quiet; nothing more;
For tales of stretching veldt,
    Kaffir and sullen Boer.

O what a lovely friend!
    O quiet easy life!
I wonder if his sister
    Would care to be my wife...

ELIZABETH JENNINGS 1926–

RELATIONSHIPS

Understanding must be on both sides,
Confidence with confidence, and every talk
Be like a long and needed walk
When flowers are picked, and almost – asides
Exchanged. Love is always like this
Even when there's no touch or kiss.

There are many kinds of relationships
But this is the best, as Plato said –
Even when it begins in a bed,
The gentle touching of hands and lips –
It is from such kindness friendship is made
Often, a thing not to be repaid

Since there is no price, no counting up
This and that, gift. Humility
Is the essential ability
Before the loved object. Oh, we can sip
Something that tastes almost divine
In such pure sharing – yours and mine.

MERLE COLLINS 1950–

SOME DAYS, MOTHER

Some days, mother
when my thoughts are a tangle I cannot untie
when meanings are lost and I cannot say why
when the daily drudging is exhausting not fulfilling
when a hollow inside says I'm existing not living
Those days, mother
when life is a circle that keeps me spinning not moving

Who else in the world could I tell of the pain?
Who else in the world would understand the hurt?
Who else in the world would I simply know is sharing?
Who else in the world could so love me in weakness?
Who else, mother? who else?

Some days, mother
when the coming of morning is an intrusion I fear
when the falling of night fuels thoughts of despair
when prayer for some deeper believing
is a passion I cannot express
when the tolling of time seems so slow
and so pointless

Who else in the world could I tell of the hurt?
Who else in the world wouldn't think me insane?
Who else in the world could love me
just for the sake of loving?
Who else, mother? Who else?

Some days, mother
when I can find no meaning
even in your existence
when we quarrel and argue
and I really wish I never knew you
when I listen and look at you

and hope I'm not seeing my future
when some other searching
has fuelled rejection

Who else in the world
would just love me again without question?
Who else holds this feeling
that nothing I do can erase?
Who else is simply always there for my story?
Who else, mother? Who else?

Some days, mother,
when I go searching for this kind of loving you're giving
when I go giving this kind of loving you're teaching
It's like trying to hold
the rainbow that drinks in the river
It's like trying to hug
the moonlight that sits on the doorstep
It's like spinning around in circles
and challenging the sky to come falling

So mother, tell me
Who else knows the secret of this deeper loving?
Who else shares the miracle of such tender caring?
Who else is there that knows
of this unstinting supporting?
Who else, mother?
Who else?

GEORGE BARKER 1913–91

TO MY MOTHER

Most near, most dear, most loved and most far,
Under the window where I often found her
Sitting as huge as Asia, seismic with laughter,
Gin and chicken helpless in her Irish hand,
Irresistible as Rabelais, but most tender for
The lame dogs and hurt birds that surround her, –
She is a procession no one can follow after
But be like a little dog following a brass band.

She will not glance up at the bomber, or condescend
To drop her gin and scuttle to a cellar,
But lean on the mahogany table like a mountain
Whom only faith can move, and so I send
O all my faith, and all my love to tell her
That she will move from mourning into morning.

SEAMUS HEANEY 1939–

from CLEARANCES III

When all the others were away at Mass
I was all hers as we peeled potatoes.
They broke the silence, let fall one by one
Like solder weeping off the soldering iron:
Cold comforts set between us, things to share
Gleaming in a bucket of clean water.
And again let fall. Little pleasant splashes
From each other's work would bring us to our senses.
So while the parish priest at her bedside
Went hammer and tongs at the prayers for the dying
And some were responding and some crying
I remembered her head bent towards my head,
Her breath in mine, our fluent dipping knives –
Never closer the whole rest of our lives.

KATHLEEN RAINE 1908–

HEIRLOOM

She gave me childhood's flowers,
Heather and wild thyme,
Eyebright and tormentil.
Lichen's mealy cup
Dry on wind-scored stone,
The corbies on the rock,
The rowan by the burn.

Sea-marvels a child beheld
Out in the fisherman's boat,
Fringed pulsing violet
Medusa, sea-gooseberries,
Starfish on the sea-floor,
Cowries and rainbow-shells
From pools on a rocky shore,

Gave me her memories,
But kept her last treasure:
'When I was a lass,' she said,
'Sitting among the heather,
'Suddenly I saw
'That all the moor was alive!
'I have told no one before.'

That was my mother's tale.
Seventy years had gone
Since she saw the living skein
Of which the world is woven,
And having seen, knew all;
Through long indifferent years
Treasuring the priceless pearl.

JOHN HEGLEY 1953–

SMOTHERING SUNDAY

To a wonderful mother
with wrinkly skin,
this card was concocted
by one of your kin.
I hope that you like it
it's specially for you,
I've sprinkled some glitter
on top of some glue.
I don't like the bought ones
I thought you should know,
they're too superficial
and two quid a throw
some of them.

'Nice warm socks,
Nice warm socks —
We should celebrate them.'

from 'The Joy of Socks'

WILLIAM CARLOS WILLIAMS 1883–1963

THIS IS JUST TO SAY

I have eaten
the plums
that were in
the icebox

and which
you were probably
saving
for breakfast

Forgive me
they were delicious
so sweet
and so cold

LI-YOUNG LEE 1957–

FROM BLOSSOMS

From blossoms comes
this brown paper bag of peaches
we bought from the boy
at the bend in the road where we turned toward
signs painted *Peaches*.

From laden boughs, from hands,
from sweet fellowship in the bins,
comes nectar at the roadside, succulent
peaches we devour, dusty skin and all,
comes the familiar dust of summer, dust we eat.

O, to take what we love inside,
to carry within us an orchard, to eat
not only the skin, but the shade,
not only the sugar, but the days, to hold
the fruit in our hands, adore it, then bite into
the round jubilance of peach.

There are days we live
as if death were nowhere
in the background; from joy
to joy to joy, from wing to wing,
from blossom to blossom to
impossible blossom, to sweet impossible blossom.

YVONNE M. FEE

FOUR O'CLOCK FANTASY

I look at you with lust – so smooth and long,
So firm, cream-filled, yet softening to my tongue,
Your sleek, smooth covering heaven to my eyes.
My conscience pricks. I know I am unwise.

Your sensuous shapeliness invades my soul
With urgent passion to consume you, whole.
In my desire to press you to my lips
I feel you slinking slowly to my hips.

It breaks my heart to leave you lying there...
'Yes – how much is that chocolate éclair?'

GLYN MAXWELL 1962–

THE PERFECT MATCH

There is nothing like the five minutes to go:
Your lads one up, your lads one down, or the whole
    Thing even. How you actually feel,
        What you truly know,
Is that your lads are going to do it. So,

However many times in the past the fact
Is that they didn't, however you screamed and strained,
    Pummelled the floor, looked up and groaned
        As the Seiko ticked
On, when the ultimate ball is nodded or kicked,

The man in the air is you. Your beautiful wife
May curl in the corner yawningly calm and true,
    But something's going on with you
        That lasts male life.
Love's one thing, but this is the Big Chief.

WENDY COPE 1945–

THE JOY OF SOCKS

Nice warm socks,
Nice warm socks—
We should celebrate them.
Ask a toe!
Toes all know
It's hard to overrate them.

Toes say, 'Please
Don't let us freeze
Till we're numb and white.
Summer's gone—
Put them on!
Wear them day and night!'

Nice warm socks,
Nice warm socks—
Who would dare to mock them?
Take good care
Of every pair
And never, ever knock them.

SYLVIA PLATH 1932–63

BALLOONS

Since Christmas they have lived with us,
Guileless and clear,
Oval soul-animals,
Taking up half the space,
Moving and rubbing on the silk

Invisible air drifts,
Giving a shriek and pop
When attacked, then scooting to rest, barely trembling.
Yellow cathead, blue fish
Such queer moons we live with

Instead of dead furniture!
Straw mats, white walls
And these travelling
Globes of thin air, red, green,
Delighting

The heart like wishes or free
Peacocks blessing
Old ground with a feather
Beaten in starry metals.
Your small

Brother is making
His balloon squeak like a cat.
Seeming to see
A funny pink world he might eat on the other side of it,
He bites,

Then sits
Back, fat jug
Contemplating a world clear as water.
A red
Shred in his little fist.

DIANE WAKOSKI 1937–

LIGHT

I live for books
and light to read them in.
                              Waterlilies
reaching up
from the depths of the pond
algae dark,
the frog loves a jell of
blue-green water,
                              the bud
scales
a rope of stem,
then floats in sunshine. Like soap
in the morning bath.
This book I read
floats in my hand like a waterlily
coming out of the nutrient waters
of thought
and light shines on us both,
the morning's breviary.

VITA SACKVILLE-WEST 1892–1962

FULL MOON

She was wearing the coral taffeta trousers
Someone had brought her from Ispahan,
And the little gold coat with pomegranate blossoms,
And the coral-hafted feather fan;
But she ran down a Kentish lane in the moonlight,
And skipped in the pool of the moon as she ran.

She cared not a rap for all the big planets,
For Betelgeuse or Aldebaran,
And all the big planets cared nothing for her,
That small impertinent charlatan;
But she climbed on a Kentish stile in the moonlight,
And laughed at the sky through the sticks of her fan.

ROBERT HERRICK (1591–1674)

UPON JULIA'S CLOTHES

Whenas in silks my Julia goes,
Then, then, methinks, how sweetly flows
That liquefaction of her clothes!

Next, when I cast mine eyes and see
That brave vibration, each way free,
– O, how that glittering taketh me!

HOWARD MOSS 1922–87

THE PERSISTENCE OF SONG

Although it is not yet evening,
The secretaries have changed their frocks
As if it were time for dancing,
And locked up in the scholars' books
There is a kind of rejoicing,
There is a kind of singing
That even the dark stone canyon makes
As though all fountains were going
At once, and the color flowed from bricks
In one wild, lit upsurging.

What is the weather doing?
And who arrived on a scallop shell
With the smell of the sea this morning?
– Creating a small upheaval
High above the scaffolding
By saying, "All will be well.
There is a kind of rejoicing."

Is there a kind of rejoicing
In saying, "All will be well"?
High above the scaffolding,
Creating a small upheaval,
The smell of the sea this morning
Arrived on a scallop shell.
What was the weather doing

In one wild, lit upsurging?
At once, the color flowed from bricks
As though all fountains were going,
And even the dark stone canyon makes
Here a kind of singing,
And there a kind of rejoicing,
And locked up in the scholars' books

There is a time for dancing
When the secretaries have changed their frocks,
And though it is not yet evening,

There is the persistence of song.

THOMAS HARDY 1840–1928

ICE ON THE HIGHWAY

Seven buxom women abreast, and arm in arm,
    Trudge down the hill, tip-toed,
        And breathing warm;
They must perforce trudge thus, to keep upright
    On the glassy ice-bound road,
And they must get to market whether or no,
    Provisions running low
        With the nearing Saturday night,
While the lumbering van wherein they mostly ride
    Can nowise go:
Yet loud their laughter as they stagger and slide!

JOHN BETJEMAN 1906–84

SEASIDE GOLF

How straight it flew, how long it flew,
   It clear'd the rutty track
And soaring, disappeared from view
   Beyond the bunker's back –
A glorious, sailing, bounding drive
That made me glad I was alive.

And down the fairway, far along
   It glowed a lonely white;
I played an iron sure and strong
   And clipp'd it out of sight,
And spite of grassy banks between
I knew I'd find it on the green.

And so I did. It lay content
   Two paces from the pin;
A steady putt and then it went
   Oh, most securely in.
The very turf rejoiced to see
That quite unprecedented three.

Ah! seaweed smells from sandy caves
   And thyme and mist in whiffs,
In-coming tide, Atlantic waves
   Slapping the sunny cliffs,
Lark song and sea sounds in the air
And splendour, splendour everywhere.

JOHN BETJEMAN 1906–84

EAST ANGLIAN BATHE

Oh when the early morning at the seaside
   Took us with hurrying steps from Horsey Mere
To see the whistling bent-grass on the leeside
   And then the tumbled breaker-line appear,
On high, the clouds with mighty adumbration
   Sailed over us to seaward fast and clear
And jellyfish in quivering isolation
   Lay silted in the dry sand of the breeze
And we, along the tableland of beach blown
   Went gooseflesh from our shoulders to our knees
And ran to catch the football, each to each thrown,
   In the soft and swirling music of the seas.

There splashed about our ankles as we waded
   Those intersecting wavelets morning-cold,
And sudden dark a patch of sea was shaded,
   And sudden light, another patch would hold
The warmth of whirling atoms in a sun-shot
   And underwater sandstorm green and gold.
So in we dived and louder than a gunshot
   Sea-water broke in fountains down the ear.
How cold the bathe, how chattering cold the drying,
   How welcoming the inland reeds appear,
The wood-smoke and the breakfast and the frying,
   And your warm freshwater ripples, Horsey Mere.

EDWARD THOMAS 1878–1917

ADLESTROP

Yes, I remember Adlestrop—
The name, because one afternoon
Of heat the express-train drew up there
Unwontedly. It was late June.

The steam hissed. Someone cleared his throat.
No one left and no one came
On the bare platform. What I saw
Was Adlestrop—only the name

And willows, willow-herb, and grass,
And meadowsweet, and haycocks dry,
No whit less still and lonely fair
Than the high cloudlets in the sky.

And for that minute a blackbird sang
Close by, and round him, mistier,
Farther and farther, all the birds
Of Oxfordshire and Gloucestershire.

FLEUR ADCOCK 1934–

AGAINST COUPLING

I write in praise of the solitary act:
of not feeling a trespassing tongue
forced into one's mouth, one's breath
smothered, nipples crushed against the
ribcage, and that metallic tingling
in the chin set off by a certain odd nerve:

unpleasure. Just to avoid those eyes would help –
such eyes as a young girl draws life from,
listening to the vegetal
rustle within her, as his gaze
stirs polypal fronds in the obscure
sea-bed of her body, and her own eyes blur.

There is much to be said for abandoning
this no longer novel exercise –
for not 'participating in
a total experience' – when
one feels like the lady in Leeds who
had seen *The Sound of Music* eighty-six times;

or more, perhaps, like the school drama mistress
producing *A Midsummer Night's Dream*
for the seventh year running, with
yet another cast from 5B.
Pyramus and Thisbe are dead, but
the hole in the wall can still be troublesome.

I advise you, then, to embrace it without
encumbrance. No need to set the scene,
dress up (or undress), make speeches.
Five minutes of solitude are
enough – in the bath, or to fill
that gap between the Sunday papers and lunch.

STEVIE SMITH 1902–71

CONVICTION

I like to get off with people,
I like to lie in their arms,
I like to be held and tightly kissed,
Safe from all alarms.

I like to laugh and be happy
With a beautiful beautiful kiss,
I tell you, in all the world
There is no bliss like this.

'My heart leaps up when I behold
A rainbow in the sky'

from 'My Heart Leaps Up When I Behold'

WILLIAM WORDSWORTH 1770–1850

MY HEART LEAPS UP WHEN I BEHOLD

My heart leaps up when I behold
  A rainbow in the sky:
So was it when my life began;
So is it now I am a man;
So be it when I shall grow old,
  Or let me die!
The Child is father of the Man;
And I could wish my days to be
Bound each to each by natural piety.

ELEANOR FARJEON 1881–1965

MORNING HAS BROKEN

Morning has broken
Like the first morning,
Blackbird has spoken
   Like the first bird.
Praise for the singing!
Praise for the morning!
Praise for them, springing
   From the first Word.

Sweet the rain's new fall
Sunlit from heaven,
Like the first dewfall
   In the first hour.
Praise for the sweetness
Of the wet garden,
Sprung in completeness
   From the first shower.

Mine is the sunlight!
Mine is the morning
Born of the one light
   Eden saw play.
Praise with elation,
Praise every morning,
Spring's re-creation
   Of the First Day!

LOUIS MACNEICE 1907–63

APPLE BLOSSOM

The first blossom was the best blossom
For the child who never had seen an orchard;
For the youth whom whisky had led astray
The morning after was the first day.

The first apple was the best apple
For Adam before he heard the sentence;
When the flaming sword endorsed the Fall
The trees were his to plant for all.

The first ocean was the best ocean
For the child from streets of doubt and litter;
For the youth for whom the skies unfurled
His first love was his first world.

But the first verdict seemed the worst verdict
When Adam and Eve were expelled from Eden;
Yet when the bitter gates clanged to
The sky beyond was just as blue.

For the next ocean is the first ocean
And the last ocean is the first ocean
And, however often the sun may rise,
A new thing dawns upon our eyes.

For the last blossom is the first blossom
And the first blossom is the best blossom
And when from Eden we take our way
The morning after is the first day.

GERARD MANLEY HOPKINS 1844–89

PIED BEAUTY

Glory be to God for dappled things –
   For skies of couple-colour as a brinded cow;
     For rose-moles all in stipple upon trout that swim;
Fresh-firecoal chestnut-falls; finches' wings;
   Landscape plotted and pieced – fold, fallow, and plough;
     And áll trádes, their gear and tackle and trim.
All things counter, original, spare, strange;
   Whatever is fickle, freckled (who knows how?)
     With swift, slow; sweet, sour; adazzle, dim;
He fathers-forth whose beauty is past change:
                    Praise him.

GERARD MANLEY HOPKINS 1844–89

SPRING

Nothing is so beautiful as spring—
    When weeds, in wheels, shoot long and lovely and lush;
    Thrush's eggs look little low heavens, and thrush
Through the echoing timber does so rinse and wring
The ear, it strikes like lightnings to hear him sing;
    The glassy peartree leaves and blooms, they brush
    The descending blue; that blue is all in a rush
With richness; the racing lambs too have fair their fling.

What is all this juice and all this joy?
    A strain of the earth's sweet being in the beginning
In Eden garden.—Have, get, before it cloy,
    Before it cloud, Christ, lord, and sour with sinning,
Innocent mind and Mayday in girl and boy,
    Most, O maid's child, thy choice and worthy the winning.

ROBERT BROWNING 1812–89

from PIPPA PASSES

The year's at the spring,
And day's at the morn;
Morning's at seven;
The hill-side's dew-pearled;
The lark's on the wing;
The snail's on the thorn:
God's in his heaven—
All's right with the world!

A.E. HOUSMAN 1859–1936

LOVELIEST OF TREES, THE CHERRY NOW

Loveliest of trees, the cherry now
Is hung with bloom along the bough,
And stands about the woodland ride
Wearing white for Eastertide.

Now, of my threescore years and ten,
Twenty will not come again,
And take from seventy springs a score,
It only leaves me fifty more.

And since to look at things in bloom
Fifty springs are little room,
Above the woodlands I will go
To see the cherry hung with snow.

ROBERT BROWNING 1812–89

HOME-THOUGHTS, FROM ABROAD

Oh, to be in England
Now that April's there,
And whoever wakes in England
Sees, some morning, unaware,
That the lowest boughs and the brushwood sheaf
Round the elm-tree bole are in tiny leaf,
While the chaffinch sings on the orchard bough
In England—now!

And after April, when May follows,
And the whitethroat builds, and all the swallows!
Hark, where my blossomed pear-tree in the hedge
Leans to the field and scatters on the clover
Blossoms and dewdrops—at the bent spray's edge—
That's the wise thrush; he sings each song twice over,
Lest you should think he never could recapture
The first fine careless rapture!
And though the fields look rough with hoary dew
All will be gay when noontide wakes anew
The buttercups, the little children's dower
—Far brighter than this gaudy melon-flower!

RUDYARD KIPLING 1865–1936

THE GLORY OF THE GARDEN

Our England is a garden that is full of stately views,
Of borders, beds and shrubberies and lawns and avenues,
With statues on the terraces and peacocks strutting by;
But the Glory of the Garden lies in more than meets the eye.

For where the old thick laurels grow, along the thin red wall,
You find the tool- and potting-sheds which are the heart of all;
The cold-frames and the hot-houses, the dungpits and the tanks,
The rollers, carts and drain-pipes, with the barrows and the planks.

And there you'll see the gardeners, the men and 'prentice boys
Told off to do as they are bid and do it without noise;
For, except when seeds are planted and we shout to scare the birds,
The Glory of the Garden it abideth not in words.

And some can pot begonias and some can bud a rose,
And some are hardly fit to trust with anything that grows;
But they can roll and trim the lawns and sift the sand and loam,
For the Glory of the Garden occupieth all who come.

Our England is a garden, and such gardens are not made
By singing: – 'Oh, how beautiful!' and sitting in the shade,
While better men than we go out and start their working lives
At grubbing weeds from gravel-paths with broken dinner-knives.

There's not a pair of legs so thin, there's not a head so thick,
There's not a hand so weak and white, nor yet a heart so sick,
But it can find some needful job that's crying to be done,
For the Glory of the Garden glorifieth every one.

Then seek your job with thankfulness and work till futher orders,
If it's only netting strawberries or killing slugs on borders;
And when your back stops aching and your hands begin to harden,
You will find yourself a partner in the Glory of the Garden.

Oh, Adam was a gardener, and God who made him sees
That half a proper gardener's work is done upon his knees,
So when your work is finished, you can wash your hands and pray
For the Glory of the Garden, that it may not pass away!
And the Glory of the Garden it shall never pass away!

ANDREW MARVELL 1621–78

from THE GARDEN

What wondrous life is this I lead!
Ripe apples drop about my head;
The luscious clusters of the vine
Upon my mouth do crush their wine;
The nectarine and curious peach
Into my hands themselves do reach;
Stumbling on melong, as I pass,
Insnared with flowers, I fall on grass.

Meanwhile the mind, from pleasure less,
Withdraws into its happiness;
The mind, that ocean where each kind
Does straight its own resemblance find;
Yet it creates, transcending these,
Far other worlds and other seas,
Annihilating all that's made
To a green thought in a green shade.

GILLIAN CLARKE 1937–

HAY-MAKING

You know the hay's in
when gates hang slack
in the lanes. These hot nights
the fallen fields lie open
under the moon's clean sheets.

The homebound road is
sweet with the liquors
of the grasses, air
green with the pastels
of stirred hayfields.

Down at Fron Felen
in the loaded barn
new bales displace
stale darknesses. Breathe.
Remember finding
first kittens, first love
in the scratch of the hay,
our sandals filled with seeds.

ANNA SEWARD 1747–1809

SONNET. DECEMBER MORNING

I love to rise ere gleams the tardy light,
Winter's pale dawn; – and as warm fires illume,
And cheerful tapers shine around the room,
Through misty windows bend my musing sight
Where, round the dusky lawn, the mansions white,
With shutters closed, peer faintly through the gloom,
That slow recedes, while yon grey spires assume,
Rising from their dark pile, an added height
By indistinctness given. – Then to decree
The grateful thoughts to God, ere they unfold
To Friendship, or the Muse, or seek with glee
Wisdom's rich page! – O, hours! more worth than gold,
By whose blest use we lengthen life, and, free
From drear decays of age, outlive the old!

JOHN CLARE 1793–1864

EMMONSAIL'S HEATH IN WINTER

I love to see the old heath's withered brake
Mingle its crimpled leaves with furze and ling,
While the old heron from the lonely lake
Starts slow and flaps its melancholy wing,
An oddling crow in idle motion swing
On the half-rotten ash-tree's topmost twig,
Beside whose trunk the gypsy makes his bed.
Up flies the bouncing woodcock from the brig
Where a black quagmire quakes beneath the tread;
The fieldfares chatter in the whistling thorn
And for the haw round fields and closen rove,
And coy bumbarrels, twenty in a drove,
Flit down the hedgerows in the frozen plain
And hang on little twigs and start again.

FAUSTIN CHARLES 1944–

LANDSCAPE

Love the land!
Feel the earth-pulse beating
In the earth-shaking Caribbean;
Worship the root-gods swelling
Mighty Silk-Cotton, poui and ginger lily
And the hibiscus trailing our destiny.
The mountain-scape swims sweetly
In the soothing river-light;
Sun panting on tree-top spotlights the caterpillar
Eating a star-apple inside out.
Caress the blue-scape, eyes peeling wide open
The bat suckling a bursting sapodilla.
When the moon is full, the crabs come out to play.
The breadfruit gives birth, bursting into rosy cheeks,
And the murmur from surrounding hills,
Hails the newborn trumpeter;
The sweet voiced bees honey the blossoms
On the shading immortelle
With an enchanting rhythm.

Love the land!
Come back to the ancient castle covered with stars,
Garlanded by birds and threaded in red wood;
The swaying cedar signals all with the melodic bamboo
Calling! calling!
When all the grasses have sprouted
And a spray of sandflies ride the leaves
And ponder the next biting session,
Listen to the night-worm gnawing the cane-root!
Listen to the golden grasshopper chirping
In the magic garden!
Listen to the cricket! Singing in the forest
Where the souls of the ancients chant through dove-calls.

Listen to the soil as it charms its children!
Return to the land!
Reclaim the children!

WILLIAM WORDSWORTH 1770–1850

COMPOSED UPON WESTMINSTER BRIDGE, SEPTEMBER 3, 1802

Earth has not anything to show more fair:
Dull would he be of soul who could pass by
A sight so touching in its majesty:
This City now doth, like a garment, wear
The beauty of the morning; silent, bare,
Ships, towers, domes, theatres, and temples lie
Open unto the fields, and to the sky;
All bright and glittering in the smokeless air.
Never did sun more beautifully steep
In his first splendour, valley, rock, or hill;
Ne'er saw I, never felt, a calm so deep!
The river glideth at his own sweet will:
Dear God! the very houses seem asleep;
And all that mighty heart is lying still!

ANDREW MOTION 1952–

IN A PERFECT WORLD

I was walking the Thames path from Richmond
to Westminster, just because I was free
to do so, just for the pleasure of light

sluicing my head, just for the breeze like a hand
tap-tapping the small of my back,
just for the slow and steady dust

fanning on bricks, on cobbles, on squared-off
slab-stones – dust which was marking the time
it takes for a thing to be born, to die,

then to be born again. The puzzled brow
of Westminster filled the distance, ducking
and diving as long parades of tree-clouds

·or skinny-ribbed office blocks worked their way
in between. The mouth of the Wandle stuck
its sick tongue out and went. The smoke-scarred walls

of a disused warehouse offered on close
inspection a locked-away world of mica
and flint and cement all hoarding the sun.

I was walking the Thames path east
as though I was water myself – each twist
and turn still bringing me out on the level,

leading me hither and thither but always
back to the hush of my clarified head,
into the chamber where one voice speaking

its mind could fathom what liberty means,
and catch the echo of others which ring
round the lip of the world. Catch and hold.

HUGH MACDIARMID 1892–1978

SCOTLAND SMALL? from DIREADH I

Scotland small? Our multiform, our infinite Scotland *small*?
Only as a patch of hillside may be a cliché corner
To a fool who cries 'Nothing but heather!' where in September
   another
Sitting there and resting and gazing round
Sees not only the heather but blaeberries
With bright green leaves and leaves already turned scarlet
Hiding ripe blue berries; and amongst the sage-green leaves
Of the bog-myrtle the golden flowers of the tormentil shining;
And on the small bare places, where the little Blackface sheep
Found grazing, milkworts blue as summer skies;
And down in neglected peat-hags, not worked
Within living memory, sphagnum moss in pastel shades
Of yellow, green, and pink; sundew and butterwort
Waiting with wide-open sticky leaves for their tiny winged prey;
And nodding harebells vying in their colour
With the blue butterflies that poise themselves delicately upon
   them;
And stunted rowans with harsh dry leaves of glorious colour.
'Nothing but heather!' – How marvellously descriptive! And
   incomplete!

'I will arise and go now, and go to Innisfree'

from 'The Lake Isle of Innisfree'

JOHN KEATS 1795–1821

from ENDYMION

A thing of beauty is a joy for ever:
Its loveliness increases; it will never
Pass into nothingness; but still will keep
A bower quiet for us, and a sleep
Full of sweet dreams, and health, and quiet breathing.
Therefore, on every morrow, are we wreathing
A flowery band to bind us to the earth,
Spite of despondence, of the inhuman dearth
Of noble natures, of the gloomy days,
Of all the unhealthy and o'er-darkened ways
Made for our searching: yes, in spite of all,
Some shape of beauty moves away the pall
From our dark spirits.

JOHN GILLESPIE MAGEE 1922–41

HIGH FLIGHT (AN AIRMAN'S ECSTASY)

Oh! I have slipped the surly bonds of Earth
And danced the skies on laughter-silvered wings;
Sunward I've climbed and joined the tumbling mirth
Of sun-split clouds – and done a hundred things
You have not dreamed of – wheeled and soared and swung
High in the sunlit silence. Hovering there,
I've chased the shouting wind along, and flung
My eager craft through footless halls of air;
Up, up the long, delirious, burning blue
I've topped the wind-swept heights with easy grace,
Where never lark or even eagle flew;
And, while with silent lifting mind I've trod
The high untrespassed sanctity of space,
Put out my hand and touched the face of God.

SIEGFRIED SASSOON 1886–1967

EVERYONE SANG

Everyone suddenly burst out singing;
And I was filled with such delight
As prisoned birds must find in freedom
Winging wildly across the white
Orchards and dark-green fields; on; on; and out of sight.

Everyone's voice was suddenly lifted,
And beauty came like the setting sun.
My heart was shaken with tears; and horror
Drifted away ... O but every one
Was a bird; and the song was wordless; the singing
    will never be done.

W.B. YEATS 1865–1939

THE LAKE ISLE OF INNISFREE

I will arise and go now, and go to Innisfree,
And a small cabin build there, of clay and wattles made:
Nine bean-rows will I have there, a hive for the honey-bee,
And live alone in the bee-loud glade.

And I shall have some peace there, for peace comes dropping slow,
Dropping from the veils of the morning to where the cricket sings;
There midnight's all a glimmer, and noon a purple glow,
And evening full of the linnet's wings.

I will arise and go now, for always night and day
I hear lake water lapping with low sounds by the shore;
While I stand on the roadway, or on the pavements grey,
I hear it in the deep heart's core.

WILLIAM WORDSWORTH 1770–1850

I WANDERED LONELY AS A CLOUD

I wandered lonely as a cloud
That floats on high o'er vales and hills,
When all at once I saw a crowd,
A host, of golden daffodils;
Beside the lake, beneath the trees,
Fluttering and dancing in the breeze.

Continuous as the stars that shine
And twinkle on the milky way,
They stretched in never-ending line
Along the margin of a bay:
Ten thousand saw I at a glance,
Tossing their heads in sprightly dance.

The waves beside them danced; but they
Outdid the sparkling waves in glee;
A poet could not but be gay,
In such a jocund company;
I gazed – and gazed – but little thought
What wealth the show to me had brought:

For oft, when on my couch I lie
In vacant or in pensive mood,
They flash upon that inward eye
Which is the bliss of solitude;
And then my heart with pleasure fills,
And dances with the daffodils.

THOM GUNN 1929–

A MAP OF THE CITY

I stand upon a hill and see
A luminous country under me,
Through which at two the drunk must weave;
The transient's pause, the sailor's leave.

I notice, looking down the hill,
Arms braced upon a window sill;
And on the web of fire escapes
Move the potential, the grey shapes.

I hold the city here, complete:
And every shape defined by light
Is mine, or corresponds to mine,
Some flickering or some steady shine.

This map is ground of my delight.
Between the limits, night by night,
I watch a malady's advance,
I recognize my love of chance.

By the recurrent lights I see
Endless potentiality,
The crowded, broken, and unfinished!
I would not have the risk diminished.

DEREK WALCOTT 1930–

THE SEASON OF PHANTASMAL PEACE

Then all the nations of birds lifted together
the huge net of the shadows of this earth
in multitudinous dialects, twittering tongues,
stitching and crossing it. They lifted up
the shadows of long pines down trackless slopes,
the shadows of glass-faced towers down evening streets,
the shadow of a frail plant on a city sill –
the net rising soundless as night, the birds' cries soundless,
    until
there was no longer dusk, or season, decline, or weather,
only this passage of phantasmal light
that not the narrowest shadow dared to sever.

And men could not see, looking up, what the wild geese drew,
what the ospreys trailed behind them in silvery ropes
that flashed in the icy sunlight; they could not hear
battalions of starlings waging peaceful cries,
bearing the net higher, covering this world
like the vines of an orchard, or a mother drawing
the trembling gauze over the trembling eyes
of a child fluttering to sleep;
                it was the light
that you will see at evening on the side of a hill
in yellow October, and no one hearing knew
what change had brought into the raven's cawing,
the killdeer's screech, the ember-circling chough
such an immense, soundless, and high concern
for the fields and cities where the birds belong,
except it was their seasonal passing, Love,
made seasonless, or, from the high privilege of their birth,
something brighter than pity for the wingless ones

below them who shared dark holes in windows and in houses,
and higher they lifted the net with soundless voices
above all change, betrayals of falling suns,
and this season lasted one moment, like the pause
between dusk and darkness, between fury and peace,
but, for such as our earth is now, it lasted long.

WILLIAM WORDSWORTH 1770–1850

from THE PRELUDE

Oh there is blessing in this gentle breeeze
That blows from the green fields and from the clouds
And from the sky; it beats against my cheek,
And seems half conscious of the joy it gives.
O welcome messenger! O welcome friend!
A captive greets thee, coming from a house
Of bondage, from yon city's walls set free,
A prison where he hath been long immured.
Now I am free, enfranchised and at large,
May fix my habitation where I will.
What dwelling shall receive me, in what vale
Shall be my harbour, underneath what grove
Shall I take up my home, and what sweet stream
Shall with its murmurs lull me to my rest?
The earth is all before me— With a heart
Joyous, nor scared at its own liberty,
I look about; and should the guide I chuse
Be nothing better than a wandering cloud
I cannot miss my way. I breathe again—
Trances of thought and mountings of the mind
Come fast upon me. It is shaken off,
As by miraculous gift 'tis shaken off,
That burthen of my own unnatural self,
The heavy weight of many a weary day
Not mine, and such as were not made for me.
Long months of peace—if such bold word accord
With any promises of human life—
Long months of ease and undisturbed delight
Are mine in prospect. Whither shall I turn,
By road or pathway, or through open field,
Or shall a twig or any floating thing
Upon the river point me out my course?
　　Enough that I am free, for months to come
May dedicate myself to chosen tasks,

May quit the tiresome sea and dwell on shore—
If not a settler on the soil, at least
To drink wild water, and to pluck green herbs,
And gather fruits fresh from their native bough.
Nay more, if I may trust myself, this hour
Hath brought a gift that consecrates my joy;
For I, methought, while the sweet breath of heaven
Was blowing on my body, felt within
A corresponding mild creative breeze,
A vital breeze which travelled gently on
O'er things which it had made, and is become
A tempest, a redundant energy,
Vexing its own creation. 'Tis a power
That does not come unrecognised, a storm,
Which, breaking up a long-continued frost,
Brings with it vernal promises, the hope
Of active days, of dignity and thought,
Of prowess in an honorable field,
Pure passions, virtue, knowledge, and delight,
The holy life of music and of verse.

E.E. CUMMINGS 1894–1962

I THANK YOU GOD

i thank You God for most this amazing
day:for the leaping greenly spirits of trees
and a blue true dream of sky;and for everything
which is natural which is infinite which is yes

(i who have died am alive again today,
and this is the sun's birthday;this is the birth
day of life and of love and wings:and of the gay
great happening illimitably earth)

how should tasting touching hearing seeing
breathing any—lifted from the no
of all nothing—human merely being
doubt unimaginable You?

(now the ears of my ears awake and
now the eyes of my eyes are opened)

STEPHEN SPENDER 1909–95

I THINK CONTINUALLY OF THOSE WHO WERE TRULY GREAT

I think continually of those who were truly great.
Who, from the womb, remembered the soul's history
Through corridors of light where the hours are suns,
Endless and singing. Whose lovely ambition
Was that their lips, still touched with fire,
Should tell of the Spirit clothed from head to foot in song.
And who hoarded from the Spring branches
The desires falling across their bodies like blossoms.

What is precious is never to forget
The essential delight of the blood drawn from ageless springs
Breaking through rocks in worlds before our earth.
Never to deny its pleasure in the morning simple light
Nor its grave evening demand for love.
Never to allow gradually the traffic to smother
With noise and fog the flowering of the spirit.

Near the snow, near the sun, in the highest fields
See how these names are fêted by the waving grass
And by the streamers of white cloud
And whispers of wind in the listening sky.
The names of those who in their lives fought for life
Who wore at their hearts the fire's centre.
Born of the sun they travelled a short while towards the sun,
And left the vivid air signed with their honour.

WILLIAM MEREDITH 1919–

ACCIDENTS OF BIRTH

Spared by a car- or airplane-crash or
cured of malignancy, people look
around with new eyes at a newly
praiseworthy world, blinking eyes like these.

For I've been brought back again from the
fine silt, the mud where our atoms lie
down for long naps. And I've also been
pardoned miraculously for years
by the lava of chance which runs down
the world's gullies, silting us back.
Here I am, brought back, set up, not yet
happened away.

But it's not this random
life only, throwing its sensual
astonishments upside down on
the bloody membranes behind my eyeballs,
not just me being here again, old
needer, looking for someone to need,
but you, up from the clay yourself,
as luck would have it, and inching
over the same little segment of earth-
ball, in the same little eon, to
meet in a room, alive in our skins,
and the whole galaxy gaping there
and the centuries whining like gnats—
you, to teach me to see it, to see
it with you, and to offer somebody
uncomprehending, impudent thanks.

ANNE FINCH, COUNTESS OF WINCHILSEA 1661–1720

ON MYSELF

Good Heav'n, I thank thee, since it was designed
I should be framed, but of the weaker kind,
That yet, my Soul, is rescued from the love
Of all those trifles which their passions move.
Pleasures and praise and plenty have with me
But their just value. If allowed they be,
Freely, and thankfully as much I taste,
As will not reason or religion waste.
If they're denied, I on myself can live,
And slight those aids unequal chance does give.
When in the sun, my wings can be displayed,
And, in retirement, I can bless the shade.

MAYA ANGELOU 1928–

PHENOMENAL WOMAN

Pretty women wonder where my secret lies.
I'm not cute or built to suit a fashion model's size
But when I start to tell them,
They think I'm telling lies.
I say,
It's in the reach of my arms,
The span of my hips,
The stride of my step,
The curl of my lips.
I'm a woman
Phenomenally.
Phenomenal woman,
That's me.

I walk into a room
Just as cool as you please.
And to a man,
The fellows stand or
Fall down on their knees.
Then they swarm around me,
A hive of honey bees.
I say,
It's the fire in my eyes,
And the flash of my teeth,
The swing in my waist,
And the joy in my feet.
I'm a woman
Phenomenally.
Phenomenal woman,
That's me.

Men themselves have wondered
What they see in me.
They try so much

But they can't touch
My inner mystery.
When I try to show them
They say they still can't see.
I say,
It's in the arch of my back,
The sun of my smile,
The ride of my breasts,
The grace of my style.
I'm a woman
Phenomenally.
Phenomenal woman,
That's me.

Now you understand
Just why my head's not bowed.
I don't shout or jump about
Or have to talk real loud.
When you see me passing
It ought to make you proud.
I say,
It's in the click of my heels,
The bend of my hair,
The palm of my hand,
The need for my care.
'Cause I'm a woman
Phenomenally.
Phenomenal woman,
That's me.

MAYA ANGELOU 1928–

STILL I RISE

You may write me down in history
With your bitter, twisted lies,
You may trod me in the very dirt
But still, like dust, I'll rise.

Does my sassiness upset you?
Why are you beset with gloom?
'Cause I walk like I've got oil wells
Pumping in my living room.

Just like moons and like suns,
With the certainty of tides,
Just like hopes springing high,
Still I'll rise.

Did you want to see me broken?
Bowed head and lowered eyes?
Shoulders falling down like teardrops,
Weakened by my soulful cries.

Does my haughtiness offend you?
Don't you take it awful hard
'Cause I laugh like I've got gold mines
Diggin' in my own back yard.

You may shoot me with your words,
You may cut me with your eyes,
You may kill me with your hatefulness,
But still, like air, I'll rise.

Does my sexiness upset you?
Does it come as a surprise
That I dance like I've got diamonds
At the meeting of my thighs?

179

Out of the huts of history's shame
I rise
Up from a past that's rooted in pain
I rise
I'm a black ocean, leaping and wide,
Welling and swelling I bear in the tide.

Leaving behind nights of terror and fear
I rise
Into a daybreak that's wondrously clear
I rise
Bringing the gifts that my ancestors gave,
I am the dream and the hope of the slave.
I rise
I rise
I rise.

ACKNOWLEDGEMENTS

— ◇ —

The publishers would like to make the following for permission to reproduce copyright material. Every effort has been made to trace copyright holders but in a few cases this has proved impossible. The publishers would be interested to hear from any copyright holders not here acknowledged.

16. 'The Body Reclining' from *Lazy Thoughts of a Lazy Woman* by Grace Nichols is reproduced with permission of Curtis Brown Ltd, London, on behalf of Grace Nichols. Copyright Grace Nichols.
18. Faber and Faber Ltd for 'The House Was Quiet and the World Was Calm' from *The Collected Poems of Wallace Stevens*.
19. 'Benediction' by James Berry is reprinted by permission of the author.
20. 'You Know What I'm Saying?' is from *Beautiful False Things* (Grove Press, 2000). Reprinted by permission of the author.
21. 'Stufferation' by Adrian Mitchell is from *Balloon Lagoon* (Orchard Books, 1997). Reprinted by permission of PFD on behalf of Adrian Mitchell. Educational Health Warning! Adrian Mitchell asks that none of his poems are used in connection to any examination whatsoever. © Adrian Mitchell 1997.
23. Bloodaxe Books for 'The Way We Live' from *Mr and Mrs Scotland Are Dead: Poems 1980–1994* by Kathleen Jamie (Bloodaxe Books, 2002).
24. 'Great Moments' by Gabriel Celaya is from *Roots and Wings: Poetry from Spain*, edited by Hardie St Martin (Harper and Row, 1976) and is translated by Robert Mezey. Reprinted by permission of Ediciones Cátedra.
27. 'Poems of Solitary Delights' by Tachibana Akemi is from *The Penguin Book of Japanese Verse* translated by Geoffrey Bownas and Anthony Thwaite (Penguin Books 1964, Revised edition 1998). Translation copyright © Geoffrey Bownas and Anthony Thwaite, 1964, 1998. Reproduced by permission of Penguin Books Ltd.
29, 135. Bloodaxe Books for 'Londoner' and 'Against Coupling' from *Poems 1960–2000* by Fleur Adcock (Bloodaxe Books, 2000).
34. Carcanet Press Ltd for 'Invocation' from 'For a Christening' from *Collected Poems* (1994) by Anne Ridler.
35. Andrew Mann Ltd for 'Transformation' from *A Time to be Born* by Jeni Couzyn (Fire Lizard, 1999). © Jeni Couzyn.
40. Carcanet Press Ltd for 'Delicious Babies' from *Selected Poems* by Penelope Shuttle (Oxford University Press, 1998).
45, 124. Faber and Faber Ltd for 'You're' and 'Balloons' from *Collected Poems* by Sylvia Plath.
46. 'The Month of June: 13 ½ is from *The Sign of Saturn* by Sharon Olds published by Secker & Warburg. Used by permission of The Random House Group Limited.

52. David Higham Associates for 'Poem in October' from *The Collected Poems* by Dylan Thomas (J.M. Dent).
57. Carcanet Press Ltd for 'Getting Older' from *Collected Poems* (2002) by Elaine Feinstein.
58. 'A Joy to be Old' is from *Selected Poems 1967–1987* by Roger McGough, published by Cape, 1989. Reprinted by permission of PFD on behalf of Roger McGough. © Roger McGough 1989.
59. 'Rondel' is from *The Collected Poems of Muriel Rukeyser* (McGraw-Hill, 1998). Copyright © 1979 by William Rukeyser. Reprinted by permission of International Creative Management, Inc.
60, 69. 'Warning' and 'The Sun Has Burst the Sky' are from *Selected Poems* by Jenny Joseph (Bloodaxe Books, 1992). Reprinted by permission of John Johnson Ltd.
61. 'Scintillate' is from *Waving at Trains* by Roger McGough, published by Cape, 1982. Reprinted by permission of PFD on behalf of Roger McGough. © Roger McGough 1982.
64. Bloodaxe Books for the extract from *Requiem: Poems 1935–1940* by Anna Akhmatova, translated by Richard McKane, from *Selected Poems* (Bloodaxe Books, 1989).
67, 114. 'Amo Ergo Sum' and 'Heirloom' are from *Collected Poems* by Kathleen Raine (Golgonooza Press, 2001). Reprinted by permission of the author.
70. 'Love Is ...' is from *Collected Poems – Adrian Henri* (Allison & Busby). Copyright © Adrian Henri 1987. Reproduced by permission of the author c/o Rogers, Coleridge and White, 20 Powis Mews, London W11 1JN.
73, 173. 'i carry your heart with me' and 'i thank You God' are reprinted from *Complete Poems 1904–1962* by E.E. Cummings, edited by George J. Firmage, by permission of W.W. Norton & Company. Copyright © 1991 by the Trustees for the E.E. Cummings Trust and George James Firmage.
74. Faber and Faber Ltd for 'As Sweet' from *Serious Concerns* by Wendy Cope.
81. David Higham Associates for 'Harlem Night Song' from *Collected Poems* by Langston Hughes (Knopf).
82. 'Wedding' is from *The Thing in the Gap-Stone Stile* by Alice Oswald. Reprinted by permission of PFD on behalf of Alice Oswald. © Alice Oswald.
83. Faber and Faber Ltd for 'The Confirmation' from *Collected Poems* by Edwin Muir.
88. HarperCollins Publishers (Australia) for 'Because She Would Ask Me Why I Loved Her' from *The Verse of Christopher Brennan* (Angus and Robertson, 1960).
90. Faber and Faber Ltd for 'My Lover' from *Making Cocoa for Kingsley Amis* by Wendy Cope.
96. Andre Deutsch for 'A Word to Husbands' from *I Wouldn't Have Missed It* by Ogden Nash.
97. Faber and Faber Ltd for 'A Dedication to My Wife' from *Collected Poems 1909–1962* by T.S. Eliot.

98. Pollinger Ltd and the Estate of Frieda Lawrence Ravagli for the extract from 'Fidelity' from *The Complete Poems of D.H.Lawrence*.

101, 137. The Estate of James MacGibbon for 'The Pleasures of Friendship' and 'Conviction' by Stevie Smith.

102. David Higham Associates for 'Friendship' from *Collected Poems* by Elizabeth Jennings (Carcanet Press Ltd).

103. 'Friendship'. Words and Music by Cole Porter. © 1939 Chappell & Co Inc, USA. Warner/Chappell Music Ltd, London W6 8BS. Reproduced by permission of International Music Publications Ltd. All rights reserved.

107. The Society of Authors as the Literary Representative of the Estate of John Masefield for 'Being Her Friend' by John Masefield.

108. The Ivor Gurney Trust for 'Companion – North-East Dug-Out' by Ivor Gurney.

109. David Higham Associates for 'Relationships' from *Relationships* by Elizabeth Jennings (Macmillan).

110. Time Warner Books UK for 'Some Days, Mother' from *Rotten Pomerack* by Merle Collins (Virago Press, 1992).

112. Faber and Faber Ltd for 'To My Mother' from *Collected Poems* by George Barker.

113. Faber and Faber Ltd for the extract from 'Clearances III' from *The Haw Lantern* by Seamus Heaney.

115. 'Smothering Sunday' is from *The Family Pack* by John Hegley, published by Methuen, 1997. Reprinted by permission of PFD on behalf of John Hegley. © John Hegley 1986, 1991, 1994, 1996.

119. Carcanet Press Ltd for 'This Is Just to Say' from *Collected Poems* (2000) by William Carlos Williams.

120. 'From Blossoms' is from *Rose* by Li-Young Lee. Copyright © 1986 by Li-Young Lee. Reprinted with the permission of BOA Editions, Ltd.

121. Fatchance Press for 'Four O'Clock Fantasy' by Yvonne M. Fee.

122. 'The Perfect Match' is from *Out of the Rain* by Glyn Maxwell. Reprinted by permission of the author.

123. 'The Joy of Socks' by Wendy Cope is reprinted by permission of the author.

126. 'Light' Copyright © 1988 by Diane Wakoski. Reprinted from *Emerald Ice: Selected Poems 1962–1987* with the permission of Black Sparrow Press.

127. 'Full Moon' by Vita Sackville-West is reproduced with permission of Curtis Brown Group, London on behalf of the Estate of Vita Sackville-West. Copyright © Vita Sackville-West 1921.

129. 'The Persistence of Song' is from *Selected Poems* by Howard Moss, published by Atheneum Publishers, New York, 1971. Copyright © 1971 by Howard Moss. Reprinted with the permission of the Estate of Howard Moss.

132, 133. John Murray (Publishers) Ltd for 'Seaside Golf' and 'East Anglian Bathe' from *Collected Poems* by John Betjeman.

142. David Higham Associates for 'Morning Has Broken' from *Blackbird Has*

Spoken by Eleanor Farjeon (Macmillan Children's Books).
143. David Higham Associates for 'Apple Blossom' from *Collected Poems* by Louis MacNeice (Faber and Faber).
147. The Society of Authors as the Literary Representative of the Estate of A.E. Housman for 'Loveliest of Trees, the Cherry Now' by A.E. Housman.
149. A.P. Watt on behalf of the National Trust for Places of Historic Interest or Natural Beauty for 'The Glory of the Garden' from *Rudyard Kipling's Verse: Definitive Edition*.
152. Carcanet Press Ltd for 'Hay-making' from *Collected Poems* (1997) by Gillian Clarke.
155. Bogle L'Ouverture Press for 'Landscape' from *Days and Nights in the Magic Forest* by Faustin Charles.
158. Faber and Faber Ltd for 'In a Perfect World' from *Public Property* by Andrew Motion.
160. Carcanet Press Ltd for 'Scotland Small?' from 'Direadh I' from *Complete Poems* (2000) by Hugh MacDiarmid.
164. 'High Flight (an Airman's Ecstasy)' by John Magee is from *John Magee, The Pilot Poet*, published by This England, Cheltenham.
165. 'Everyone Sang' by Siegfried Sassoon. Copyright Siegfried Sassoon by permission of George Sassoon.
166. A.P. Watt on behalf of Michael B. Yeats for 'The Lake Isle of Innisfree' from *The Collected Poems of W.B. Yeats*.
168. Faber and Faber Ltd for 'A Map of the City' from *Selected Poems* by Thom Gunn.
169. Faber and Faber Ltd for 'The Season of Phantasmal Peace' from *Collected Poems* by Derek Walcott.
174. Faber and Faber Ltd for 'I Think Continually of Those Who Were Truly Great' from *Collected Poems* by Stephen Spender.
175. 'Accidents of Birth' is from *The Cheer* by William Meredith (Alfred A. Knopf, 1980).
177, 179. Time Warner Books UK for 'Phenomenal Woman' and 'Still I Rise' from *And Still I Rise* by Maya Angelou (Virago Press).

INDEX OF POETS' NAMES

— ◇ —

INDEX OF FIRST LINES

— ◇ —